# Matthew Henry's Sermon Outlines

# THE WORLD'S GREAT SERMONS IN OUTLINE

*Selected and Edited by*
SHELDON B. QUINCER

*The World's Great Sermons in Outline*

# Matthew Henry's
# SERMON OUTLINES

## A CHOICE COLLECTION OF THIRTY-FIVE MODEL SERMONS

*by*

## MATTHEW HENRY

**Author of the Famous**
**MATTHEW HENRY COMMENTARY**

*Selected and Edited by*

SHELDON B. QUINCER, D.D.
Baptist Theological Seminary
Grand Rapids, Michigan

WM. B. EERDMANS PUBLISHING COMPANY
Grand Rapids                                          Michigan

*Reprinted, January 1982*

ISBN 0-8028-1155-8

PHOTOLITHOPRINTED BY EERDMANS PRINTING COMPANY
GRAND RAPIDS, MICHIGAN, UNITED STATES OF AMERICA

# Foreword

Some of the greatest preachers the world has ever known were the godly ministers of the Word of past generations. Among these was Matthew Henry. While he has been known and loved for two centuries for his devotional commentary on the whole Bible, it has not been so generally known that he was a distinguished preacher.

He was born in Wales in 1662 and began his preaching ministry at the age of twenty-four. About two years later he was ordained and entered the active pastorate, serving the Chester Presbyterian Church. He served this congregation for twenty-five years. From Chester he accepted a call to London where he ended his active pastoral duties in 1714 when called to higher service in the heavenly kingdom.

The greatness of Matthew Henry's sermons consists in their Scriptural content, lucid presentation, practical application, and Christ-centeredness. Someone has described him: "Like the Apostle Paul, whom he admired more than all mere mortals and whom he has signalized as 'the most active, zealous servant that ever our Master had,' he daily studied to know nothing 'save Jesus Christ and Him crucified.'"[1]

These sermon outlines have been taken and edited from *The Miscellaneous Works of the Reverend Matthew Henry* (2 volumes) and from his devotional commentary, *An Exposition of the Old and New Testaments* (5 volumes).

SHELDON B. QUINCER

Grand Rapids, Mich.
February, 1955

————

1. Miscellaneous Works of the Reverend Matthew Henry, vol. i, p. vi.

# Contents

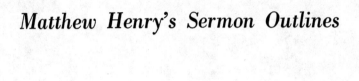

*Matthew Henry's Sermon Outlines*

# 1

# A Memorial to the Fire of the Lord

*And he called the name of the place Ta-
berah, because the fire of the Lord burnt
among them.*        —Numbers 11:3

W E HAVE here an account of the prudent and pious
care which Moses took to preserve the memorial of a fire which
happened in the camp of Israel by giving a new name of suitable
signification to the place where it happened, which being left upon
record here in the book of God is a monument of the fire further
visible and more desirable than their pillar of stone; for wherever
the books of Moses are read, there shall this be told for a memorial.

## I. THE JUDGMENT OF GOD UPON ISRAEL.

A. **The Nature of the Judgment.** It is called the fire of the
   Lord because it fell from heaven; it came immediately from
   the hand of God.  Here it consumed the sinners to signify
   that their iniquity was such as should not be purged with
   sacrifice or offering forever, as another time it consumed the
   sacrificers when they offered strange fires.

B. **The People of the Judgment.** The fire of the Lord burned
   among the people whom God favored when by sin they displeased Him and His anger was kindled against them.  Though
   the pillar of cloud and fire was over them to protect them
   while they kept themselves in the love of God, that should be
   no security to them when they rebelled against Him.

C. **The Cause of the Judgment.** The people complained; that
   was it which provoked God to kindle His fire among them.
   Those who are always complaining about trifles must expect
   to have something given to them to complain about.  Nothing

11

is more displeasing to God than our being displeased at His disposals.

## II THE MEMORIAL OF THE JUDGMENT OF GOD UPON ISRAEL.

A. **The Purpose of the Memorial in Relation to Israel.** The fire of the Lord must not be forgotten; he therefore calls the place Taberah — a burning. And if posterity ask, "What burning?" it will be answered, "The burning of a part of the camp of the Israelites with the fire of the Lord for their discontent and murmuring."

B. **The Purpose of the Memorial in Relation to Us.** By recording these things in His sacred writings God has more effectually preserved the memorial of them and transmitted it even to us.

1. *Personal rebukes.* We must often call to mind the personal and private rebukes of Providence which we and our families have been under. We should remember what God has spoken not only by His Word, but also by His rod. We should remember them in order to renew our repentance for the sins that produced them.

2. *Public judgments.* We must call to mind public judgments upon the communities of which we are members; upon the land and nation, God's controversies with them; upon the city, His voice that has cried to it; for as in the peace thereof we have peace, so in the trouble thereof we have trouble and must feel it.

## III. THE LESSONS FROM THE JUDGMENT OF GOD UPON ISRAEL.

A. **God is Terrible in His Judgments.** See how terrible God is in His judgments and fear before Him. If the glory of His greatness be like fire to a people who are entering into covenant with Him, much more will the terror of His wrath be so to a people who have broken covenant with Him.

B. **Sin is a Mischievous Thing.** Sin provokes God to be our enemy and to fight against us. He never contends with a people, but it is sin that is the cause of the controversy. National sins bring national judgments. The sins of a city bring misery upon it. It was the wickedness of Sodom that made it combustible matter for the fire of God's wrath.

C. **This World is an Uncertain Thing.** This is seen in Job whom the rising sun found the richest of men and the setting sun left poor to a proverb. Our Savior speaks of the danger we are in of losing our treasures upon earth by the moth that corrupts or thieves that break through and steal (Matthew 6:19).

D. **God Remembers Mercy in the Midst of Wrath.** When the fire of the Lord burned in the camp of Israel Moses prayed and then the fire was quenched. The prophet Amos tells us that when in his time the Lord called to contend by fire he prayed, "O Lord God, cease I beseech Thee," and "the Lord repented for this: this shall not be, saith the Lord God" (Amos 7:4-6).

E. **Man is Dependent upon God for Safety.** "Except the Lord keep the city, the watchman waketh but in vain." It is therefore your great concern to make Him your friend and to keep yourselves in His love; to secure the favor of the Ruler of rulers from whom every man's judgment proceeds. He has put you into an easy way of doing this, not by costly sacrifices and offerings, but by faithful and earnest prayer, kept up in its life and not sunk into a formality.

F. **The Great Day of the Lord will be a Dreadful Day.** See what a dreadful day the great day of the Lord will be when the world shall be on fire and the earth and all the works that are therein shall be burnt up. When the heavens being on fire shall be dissolved and the elements shall melt with fervent heat and all these things shall be dissolved (II Peter 3:11-12).

## CONCLUSION

There is a fire yet more dreadful. The earth and the works that are therein will soon be burned up; but there is a lake of fire which burns eternally and shall never be quenched into which all the wicked and ungodly shall be cast by the irreversible sentence of the righteous Judge and in which they shall be tormented without end. Flee from wrath to come by fleeing from sin to Christ that you come not to the place of torment.

# 2

# *A Two-fold Prayer*

> *O let the wickedness of the wicked come to an end; but establish the just.*
> —Psalm 7:9

W E ARE here taught to pray against all sin. And in praying against sin we pray for the sinners; for whatever works against the disease, works for the patient. We are also taught to pray for all saints. Let not those who are filthy be filthy still, but let those who are holy be holy still. Let the good be kept so and made better.

## I. THE CONTENT OF THE PRAYER.

A. The Petition that God Will Bring the Wickedness of the Wicked to an End. We must pray that God will bring our own wickedness and the wickedness of other people to an end.

1. *Abandonment of wicked principles.* It must be our heart's desire and prayer that wicked principles may be exploded and abandoned and that men may be set right in their judgments concerning good and evil, right and wrong, God and themselves, this world and the other.

2. *Conversion of the wicked.* Let us be humbly earnest with God in prayer that the eyes of the spiritually blind may be opened; and the ears of the deaf unstopped; that wandering sheep may be sought and saved and prodigal sons brought to themselves and then to the Father's house; that God will translate those into the kingdom of His dear Son who have been long subjects in the kingdom of darkness.

3. *Prevention and restraining of wicked practices.* We must desire and pray that wicked practices may be prevented

14

and restrained; that if the stream be not turned, yet it may
be checked and may not become an over-flowing deluge. We
should desire and pray that thus far, at least, the wickedness
of the wicked come to an end, that it may not be committed
openly and that the infection may not spread.

B. The Petition that God Will Establish the Just.

1. *In integrity.* Let us pray that the just may be established
   in their good principles and good resolutions and may
   faithfully adhere to them; that those who have clean hands
   may be stronger and stronger; though the stream be strong,
   that the righteous may never be carried down by it; that
   like Job in difficult and trying times they may hold forth
   their integrity.

2. *In comfort and hope.* In troublesome times good men are
   apt to be shaken in mind and to fear lest the cause and
   interest of Christianity should be sunk and rundown. They
   are ready to give up all for gone. Therefore, we have need
   to pray for them that they may be established in the belief
   of the promise that the gates of hell shall never prevail
   against the church.

3. *In the saints' undertaking to bring wickedness to an end.*
   Pray that they may be established in their undertaking
   to do what they can to bring the wickedness of the wicked
   to an end. We ought to pray for civil rulers; for all
   ministers of the Word of God; for all who in their places
   are strong against sin that they may be established in their
   resolution not to draw back their hand from the battle
   against sin.

## II. THE REASON FOR THE PRAYER.

A. A Holy Concern for the Honor of God. All good people
have a holy concern for the name and honor of God and the
Lord Jesus and for the reputation of Christianity. Therefore,
they cannot but desire the end of that which dishonors God.
All the children of God having His glory as their highest end

have it upon their hearts as their chief care, and it is dearer to them than any interests of their own.

1. *It is the saints' highest end.*

2. *It is the saints' chief care.*

B. **A Tender Love for the Souls of Men.** The children of God have a tender love for the souls of men and a true desire of their welfare here and hereafter; and therefore they cannot but desire and pray for the ending of that which ruins souls.

1. *The value of a soul.* You know for what they were and in whose image they were made; for what they were bought and with what price they were bought; what service for God they are capable of doing; what happiness in God they are capable of enjoying.

2. *The natural condition of the soul.* It is alienated from its rightful Lord and sold for a mess of pottage, for the gratifications of a base lust, into the hands of a sworn enemy and made a prey to the roaring lion. Here is one made a cage of unclean and filthy birds who is capable of being made a temple of the Holy Spirit; a drudge of Satan who might have been a servant of God; an instrument of unrighteousness who might have been a vessel of honor.

C. **A Great Value for the Grace of God.**

1. *The power of grace.* All good people have a great value for the grace of God and are convinced of the sovereignty and power, the necessity and efficacy of that grace; and therefore, they pray for that grace, both for the reformation of sinners and for the establishment of the just. They know that nothing can be done without it and whatever good they wish to be effected, either upon saints or sinners, they depend upon that grace for it and its powerful influences.

2. *The promise of grace.* They know also that this grace is promised to the church, this clean water to cleanse it from all filthiness and from all of its idols. Yet God will be inquired of by His people, to do it for them; we must ask and then we shall receive.

## CONCLUSION

Let us do what we can to bring the wickedness of the wicked to an end. Let our conduct in everything be such as becomes the gospel of Christ, strict and conscientious. Let us do what we can to establish the just, to confirm the good in their goodness. Let those who fear the Lord speak often one to another for instruction, quickening, and encouragement.

# 3

# A Song of Comfort

> *The Lord is my Shepherd; I shall not want.*
> *He maketh me to lie down in green pas-*
> *tures: He leadeth me beside the still wa-*
> *ters. He restoreth my soul: He leadeth me*
> *in the paths of righteousness for His name's*
> *sake. Yea, though I walk through the val-*
> *ley of the shadow of death, I will fear no*
> *evil: for Thou art with me; Thy rod and*
> *Thy staff they comfort me. Thou preparest*
> *a table before me in the presence of mine*
> *enemies: Thou anointest my head with oil,*
> *my cup runneth over. Surely goodness and*
> *mercy shall follow me all the days of my*
> *life, and I will dwell in the house of the*
> *Lord forever.* —Psalm 23

IT IS the duty of Christians to encourage themselves in the Lord their God; and we are here directed to take that encouragement both from the relation wherein He stands to us and from the expectation we have had of His goodness, according to that relation.

## I. THE COMFORT OF PROVISION. Verse 1

### A. God's Care of Believers: "the Lord is my Shepherd."

1. *This is seen in that the Lord is called a shepherd.* He is their Shepherd and they may call Him so. There was a time when David was a shepherd (Psalm 78:70-71); so he knew by experience the cares and tender affections of a good shepherd toward his flock.

2. *This is seen in the shepherd's responsibilities.* He that is the Shepherd of Israel is the Shepherd of every individual

believer. He takes them into His fold and then takes care
of them, protects them and provides for them with more
care and constancy than a shepherd can that makes it his
business to keep the flock.

B. **Believer's Confidence in God: "I shall not want."**

1. *The confidence expressed.* "If the Lord is my Shepherd,
my Feeder, I may conclude I shall not want anything that
is really necessary and good for me." Let not those fear
starving that are at God's finding and have Him for their
Feeder.

2. *The truth implied.* More is implied than is expressed. It
is not only, "I shall not want," but, "I shall be supplied with
whatever I need; and if I have not everything I desire, I
may conclude it is either not fit for me or not good for me,
or I shall have it in due time."

II. **THE COMFORT OF GOD'S PRESENCE AND PRO-
TECTION. Verses 2-4.**

A. **The Comforts of a Living Saint.**

1. *They are well pleased*: "He maketh me to lie down in green
pastures." God makes His saints to lie down; He gives
them quiet and contentment in their own minds, whatever
their lot is; their souls dwell at ease in Him and that makes
every pasture green.

2. *They are well guided*: "He leadeth me beside the still
waters." The Shepherd of Israel guides Joseph like a flock;
and every believer is under the same guidance. He leads
them by His providence, by His Word, by His Spirit. He
disposes their affairs for the best, according to His counsel.

3. *They are well helped*: "He restoreth my soul." He brings
us back when we wander. He recovers us when we are
sick and revives us when we are faint "and so restores the
soul that was ready to depart."

## B. The Courage of a Dying Saint.

1. *The supposition of imminent danger*: "Though I walk through the valley of the shadow of death." Here is one word which sounds terrible — death. But even in the supposition of distress there are four words which lessen the terror: shadow; valley; walk; through, that is, they will not be lost in this valley.

2. *The triumph over danger*: "I will fear no evil." A believer may meet death with a holy security and serenity of mind; (a) because there is no evil in it for the saint; (b) because he has God's gracious presence with him in his dying moments.

## III. THE COMFORT OF GOD'S PERPETUAL MERCY. Verses 5-6.

## A. God's Gracious Favors.

1. *A sufficient supply*: "Thou preparest a table before me." There has been provided for the children of God all things pertaining to life and godliness, all things requisite both for body and soul, time and eternity. David acknowledges that he had food sufficient.

2. *A plentiful supply*: "Thou anointest my head with oil, my cup runneth over." Plentiful provision is made for our bodies and for our souls; for the life that now is and for that which is to come. If Providence does not bestow upon us thus plentifully for our natural life, it is our own fault if it be not made up to us in spiritual blessings.

## B. Continuance of God's Favors.

1. *The personal assurance*: "Surely goodness and mercy shall follow me." It is pardoning mercy, protecting mercy, sustaining mercy, supplying mercy.

2. *The manner of conveyance of the favors*: "follow me." It shall follow us as the water out of the rock followed the camp of Israel through the wilderness; it shall follow into all places and all conditions. It shall be always ready.

3. *The constancy of the favors*: "All the days of my life." They shall follow us even to the last; for whom God loves, He loves to the end. They shall be new every morning (Lamentations 3:22-23), like the manna that was given to the Israelites daily.

4. *The certainty of the favors*: "surely." It is as sure as the promise of the God of truth can make it; and we know whom we have believed.

5. *The prospect of the perfection of joy*: "I will dwell in the house of the Lord forever." Here is a prospect of the perfection of bliss in the future state. Some understand verse 5 to mean: "Goodness and mercy having followed me all the days of my life on this earth, when that is ended, I shall remove to a better world, to dwell in the house of the Lord forever, in our Father's house above where there are many mansions."

## CONCLUSION

If God's goodness to us is like the morning light which shines more and more to the perfect day; let not ours to Him be like the morning cloud and the early dew that passes away. Those that would be satisfied with the fatness of God's house must keep close to the duties of it.

# 4

## How to Spend the Day with God

*On Thee do I wait all the day.*
—Psalm 25:5

W HICH of us can truly say the words of the text? Which of us lives this life of communion with God, which is so much our business and blessedness? Yet, David's professions in the text show us what should be our practice.

### I. A PATIENT EXPECTATION OF GOD'S MERCY.

**A. Though We Must Wait Long.** It seems long while we are kept waiting, but it is no longer than God has appointed and we are sure His time is the best time and His favors are worth waiting for.

**B. Though the Day is Dark.** Though while we are kept waiting for what God will do we are kept in the dark concerning what He is doing and what is best for us to do, yet let us be content to wait in the dark.

**C. Though the Day is Stormy.** Even though the wind be contrary and drive us back, nay, though it be boisterous, yet we must wait and weather the storm by patience. Christ is in the ship.

### II. A CONSTANT ATTENDANCE UPON GOD.

**A. The Meaning of Waiting upon God.**

1. *It is a life of desire toward God.* Our desire must be not only towards the good things that God gives, but toward God Himself, his favor and love, the manifestation of His name to us and the influences of His grace upon us.

22

2. *It is a life of delight in God.* Our delight in God must be such that we never wish for more than God. Believing Him to be the all-sufficient God we must be entirely satisfied in Him; let Him be mine and I have enough.

3. *It is a life of dependence upon God.* It is as the child who waits on his father, in whom he has confidence and on whom he casts his care. It is to expect all good to come to us from God.

4. *It is a life of devotedness to God.* To wait on God is entirely and unreservedly to refer ourselves to His wise and holy directions and disposals and cheerfully to acquiesce in them and comply with them.

B. The Time of Waiting upon God.

1. *It is every day.* We must wait on God every day; on the Lord's day and on weekdays; on idle days and on busy days; in days of prosperity and in days of adversity; in the day of youth and in the days of old age.

2. *It is all the day.* We must cast our daily cares upon God and manage our daily business for Him; receive our daily comforts from Him and resist our daily temptations and do our daily duties in His strength; and bear our daily afflictions with submission to His will.

III. PRACTICAL REMINDERS FOR WAITING UPON GOD.

A. The Duty of Waiting upon God.

1. *In behalf of the family.* When you meet with your families in the morning, wait upon God for a blessing upon them and render thanks for the mercies received. In the education of your children wait upon God to make their education successful.

2. *In behalf of ourselves.* Wait upon God in behalf of your business, in reading, at meal time, when visiting, in your charity, and when journeying; when alone as a guard against temptation.

**B. The Motives for Waiting upon God.**

1. *The eye of God upon us.* He sees all the motions of our hearts and sees with pleasure the motions of our hearts towards Him. This should lead us to set Him always before us.

2. *The knowledge of God.* "All things," even the thoughts and intents of the heart, "are naked and opened unto the eyes of Him with whom we have to do" (Hebrews 4:13). And we must give an account of ourselves to Him.

3. *The graciousness of God.* He continually waits to be gracious to us; He is always doing us good. He daily loads us with His benefits. His good providence waits on us all the day to preserve our going out and our coming in.

4. *The ministry of holy angels.* They are all appointed to be ministering spirits to minister for the good of them who shall be heirs of salvation (Hebrews 1:14) and more good offices they do us every day than we are aware.

5. *It is heaven upon earth.* This life of communion with God is a heaven upon earth. It is an earnest of the blessedness of heaven and a preparative for it.

**C. The Directions for Waiting upon God.**

1. *See God in creation.* Look about you and see what a variety of wonders, what an abundance of comforts, with which you are surrounded and let them lead you to Him Who is the Giver of all good.

2. *See the nothingness of a creature without God.* The more we discern of the vanity and emptiness of the world and all our enjoyments in it and their utter insufficiency to make us happy, the closer we shall cleave to God and the more intimately we shall converse with Him.

3. *Live by faith in the Lord Jesus.* We cannot with any confidence wait upon God but in and through a Mediator. It is by His Son that God speaks to us and hears from us. All that passes between God and man must pass through that Daysman.

4. *Be frequent and serious in pious ejaculations.* It is not the length or language of prayer that God looks at, but the sincerity of the heart in it; and that shall be accepted, though the prayer be short and the groanings such as cannot be uttered.

5. *Look upon every day as the last day.* Although we cannot say that we ought to live as if we were sure this day would be our last, yet it is certain we ought to live as those who do not know but it may be so. If we thought more of death we would converse more with God.

## CONCLUSION

If we continue waiting on God every day and all the day long, we shall grow more experienced and consequently more expert in communion with God. "Turn thou to thy God; keep mercy and judgment, and wait on thy God continually" (Hosea 12:6).

# 5

# A Thanksgiving Sermon

*Thou crownest the year with thy goodness.*
—Psalm 65:11

LET the feast of Thanksgiving be kept to the honor of
that God who is the Alpha and Omega, the First and the Last;
both the spring and center of all our glories. For of Him and
through Him and to Him are all things. To Him must the vow
of thanksgiving be performed for His mercies to the land of our
nativity. And how can we sum up our acknowledgements of God's
favors to our nation in more proper moods than those of the text?

## I. COMMON PROVIDENCE CROWNS EVERY YEAR WITH GOD'S GOODNESS.

A. **The Regular Succession of the Seasons.** Summer and
winter crown the year; God made both, and both for the
service of men. God's covenant with Noah and his sons
(Genesis 8:22) by which the seasons of the year were re-
settled after the interruption of the deluge is the crown and
glory of every year; and the constant and regular succession
of summer and winter, seed-time and harvest, in performance
of that promise, is an encouragement to our faith in the covenant of grace, which is established as firmly as those ordi-
nances of heaven.

B. **The Fruits and the Products of the Earth.** The annual
fruits and products of the earth, grass for the cattle and herbs
for the service of men — with these the earth is every year
enriched for use; as well as beautified and adorned for show.
The harvest is the crown of every year and the great influence
of God's goodness to an evil and unthankful world. And so
kind and bountiful is the hand of Providence herein that we

26

are supplied not only with food, but with a variety of pleasant
things for ornament and delight.

## II. SPECIAL PROVIDENCES CROWN SOME YEARS WITH GOD'S GOODNESS MORE THAN OTHERS.

A. **Illustration from Jewish History.** Every year was
crowned with God's goodness, but not to the extent of the
sixth year when God made the earth to bring forth fruit for
three years (Psalm 77:10). Every year was not a year of
release, much less a year of jubilee. Sometimes the arm of
Omnipotence is in a special manner made bare and He outdoes
what He used to do that He may awaken a stupid and un-
thinking world to see the goings of our God in His sanctuary
and that He may proclaim Himself glorious in holiness, fearful
in praises, working wonders.

B. **Practical Observation.** God's goodness must be recognized
and acknowledged. Whatever has been or is our honor, our
joy, our hope comes from God's hand and He must have the
praise for it. We must take notice, not only of His wisdom
and power in effecting things great and admirable in themselves, but His goodness and mercy in doing that which is
happy and advantageous for us; and make that the theme of
all of our songs. "For He is good: for His mercy endureth
forever" (Psalm 136:1).

C. **The Description of God's Goodness.** A crown signifies
three things:

1. *It dignifies and adorns.* A crown denotes honor.

2. *It surrounds and encloses.* God has surrounded this year
with His goodness, compassed and enclosed it on every side.
So is translated the same word in Psalm 5:12: "With favor
wilt thou *compass* (crown) him as with a shield."

3. *It finishes and completes.* God has crowned, that is, He
has finished the year with His goodness. The happy issue
of an affair we call the crown of it.

## III. MAN'S RESPONSIBILITY TO GOD FOR HIS GOODNESS.

A. **To Praise God.** Let us cast all the crowns of the blessings of the year at His feet by our humble, grateful acknowledgement of His infinite wisdom, power, and mercy. Let our closets and families witness to our constant pious adorations of the divine greatness and devout acknowledgements of the divine goodness to us and to our land; that every day may be with us a thanksgiving day and we may live a life of praise (Psalms 145:2; 119:164). Those who thus honor God no doubt He will yet further honor.

B. **To Repent of Sin.** Let the goodness of God lead us to repentance and engage us all to reform our lives, to be more watchful of sin, and to abound more in the service of God and in everything that is virtuous and praiseworthy. Then, and then only, we offer praise so as to indeed glorify God when we order our conduct aright; and then shall we be sure to see His great salvation and be forever praising Him.

C. **To Increase our Goodness to One Another.** It is justly expected that they who obtain mercy should show mercy and so reflect the rays of the divine goodness upon all about them; being herein "followers of God as dear children" (Ephesians 5:1), "followers of Him that is good" (I Peter 3:13) in His goodness. Let God's goodness to us constrain us, as we have opportunity, to do good to all men; to do good with what we have in the world, as faithful stewards of the manifold grace of God; to do good with all the abilities God gives us.

D. **To Support and Encourage our Expectations for Next Year.** Has God crowned us with His goodness this year? Let us thence infer that if we approve ourselves faithful to God surely goodness and mercy shall still follow us. And our hopes ought to be the matter of our praises as well as our joys (Psalm 75:1). The wondrous works for which we are giving thanks this day are upon this account the more valuable in that they give us ground to hope that God's name is near, and in the accomplishments of His promise.

## CONCLUSION

That comprehensive prayer, "Father glorify Thy name," has already obtained an answer from heaven — which true believers may apply to themselves — "I have both glorified it, and will glorify it again" (John 12:28). May the goodness and mercy of God so lavishly bestowed upon us as individuals and as a nation not only lead us to proclaim His praise orally, but to show forth our gratitude in lives surrendered to Him who is the giver of every good and perfect gift (James 1:17).

# 6

## Hope and Fear Balanced

*The Lord taketh pleasure in them that*
*fear him, in those that hope in his mercy.*
—Psalm 147:11

THE favorites of God are those who fear Him and hope
in His mercy. A holy fear of God must be a check upon our hope
to keep us from presumption and a pious hope in God must be a
check on our fear to keep us from sinking into despondency.

## I. THERE MUST BE A BALANCED FEAR AND HOPE CONCERNING OUR SPIRITUAL LIFE.

A. **We Must Have a Holy Dread of God and a Humble Delight in Him.** We should keep up a reverence of God's majesty with a fear of incurring His displeasure and at the same time a joy in His love and grace, and an entire complacency in His beauty and bounty and benignity.

1. *Reverence for God's majesty.*

2. *Joy in God's love and grace.*

B. **We Must Tremble for Sin and Triumph in Christ.** We must be afraid of the curse and the terrors of sin, but rejoice in the covenant and the riches and graces of it.

1. *Fear the curse and terrors of sin.* We must look upon sin and be humbled and afraid of God's wrath.

2. *Rejoice in the riches and graces of God's covenant.* We must look upon Christ and be satisfied and hope in His mercy.

C. **We Must Have a Jealousy of Ourselves and a Grateful Sense of God's Grace in Us.**

1. *The deceitfulness of the human heart.* The heart of man is deceitful above all things. We have, therefore, reason to fear lest we should be mistaken and rejected as hypocrites.

30

2. *The grace of God in us.* Let not those who fear the Lord walk in darkness, but trust in the name of the Lord and stay themselves upon their God.

D. We Must Keep a Constant Caution over our Ways and a Constant Confidence in the Grace of God.

   1. *Man's weakness.* When we consider how weak we are we shall see cause enough to walk humbly with God. We have need to stand always on our guard.

   2. *Man's hope in God's mercy.* In the midst of the fear we must hope in God's mercy, that He will take our part against our spiritual enemies and watch over us for good.

E. We Must Have a Holy Fear lest We Come Short and a Good Hope that through Grace We Will Persevere.

   1. *Man's unworthiness.* When we look upon the brightness of the crown set before us and our own meanness and unworthiness and the many difficulties, we may justly be afraid.

   2. *God's faithfulness.* If it be the work of God's hands He will not forsake it, He will perfect it. "He is faithful that promised" (Hebrews 10:23).

II. THERE MUST BE A BALANCED HOPE AND FEAR CONCERNING OUR TEMPORAL LIFE.

A. In Seasons of Prosperity.

   1. *Recognize the sovereignty of the Divine Providence.* We are in His hands as clay is in the hand of the potter to be formed, unformed, new-formed as He pleases.

   2. *Recognize the vanity of the world.* There are no pleasures here below that are lasting, but they are all dying things. They are as flowers which soon fade.

   3. *Recognize that we are undeserving and ill-deserving.* We shall see a great deal of reason not to be confident of our creature-comforts when we consider that we are not worthy of them and much less worthy to have them secured to us.

   4. *Recognize that trouble and changes should be expected.* Keep up a lively expectation of troubles and changes in this

changeable, troublesome world. They are good for us, lest we grow proud and secure and in love with this world.

5. *Recognize the approach of death.* Though the comforts we enjoy should not be taken from us, though we were ever so sure they would not, yet we know not how soon we may be taken from them.

B. In Seasons of Distress.

1. *Hope in God's power.* No matter how imminent the danger, He can prevent it; no matter how great the straits, He can extricate us out of them.

2. *Hope in God's providence.* Hope in the usual method of providence, which sets prosperity and adversity one over against the other; and when the ebb is at the lowest makes the tide to turn.

3. *Hope in God's pity and compassion.* God is gracious and merciful. He does not afflict willingly, but when there is cause and when there is need; and therefore He will not always chide.

4. *Hope in God's promise.* God has promised that nothing shall harm His followers (I Peter 3:13); all things shall work together for good to them (Romans 8:28), and shall not be able to separate them from God's love (Romans 8:39).

## III. THERE MUST BE A BALANCED HOPE AND FEAR CONCERNING THE CHURCH IN RELATION TO PUBLIC AFFAIRS.

A. We Have Reason for a Holy Fear in Regard to Public Affairs.

1. *Because we are a provoking people.* God's name is dishonored, His day profaned, His good creatures abused by luxury and excess. Liberty to sin has been pleaded for a Christian liberty.

2. *Because we are a divided people.* It is not so much the difference of sentiment and practice; but that which does

the mischief is the mismanagement of our differences and uncharitable censures one of another.

3. *Because of the presence of evil.* Let the people of God never expect, until they come to heaven, to be out of reach of evil, and therefore never expect to be perfectly quiet from the fear of it.

B. We Have Reason to Keep up Good Hope in Regard to Public Affairs.

   1. *The Word of God.* This is the foundation on which our hopes must be built and then they are fixed. See Revelation 11 :15; Psalms 2 :8; 98 :3; Micah 4 :3; Isaiah 11 :1-9.

   2. *The work of God.* The interest that lies so much upon our hearts, the progress of Christianity, is the work of His own hands which He will never forsake.

   3. *The wonders of God.* When we are discouraged let us remember the works of the Lord; not only those of which our fathers have told us, but which we have seen in our days.

## CONCLUSION

Be of good courage and hope in God; stay yourselves upon Him, strengthen yourselves in Him, look upwards with cheerfulness, and then look forward with satisfaction.

# 7

# The Pleasantness of the Godly Life

*Her ways are ways of pleasantness, and
all her paths are peace.*

—Proverbs 3:17

T RUE religion and godliness is often in Scripture, and
particularly in the book of Proverbs, represented and recommended
to us under the name and character of wisdom. The text reveals
that true piety has true pleasure in it.

## I. THE CHARACTER OF THE PLEASANTNESS OF THE GODLY LIFE.

### A. It is Real and Not Counterfeit.

1. *The counterfeit pleasures.* Carnal worldlings pretend a great
satisfaction in the enjoyments of the world and the gratifica-
tion of sense; but "the end of that mirth is heaviness" and
in that "laughter the heart is sorrowful."

2. *The genuine pleasures.* The pleasures of the godly life are
solid, substantial pleasures and not painted; gold and not
gilded over; these sons of pleasure "inherit substance." They
have, like their Master, "meat to eat which the world knows
not of."

### B. It is Rational and Not Brutish.

1. *The pleasures of the soul.* The pleasures of godliness are
not those of the mere animal life which arise from the
gratifications of the senses of the body and its appetites; no,
they affect the soul. They are of a spiritual nature and
satisfy.

34

2. *The pleasures of sense.* The brute creatures have the same pleasures of sense that we have; but what are those to man who is "taught more than the beasts of the earth and made wiser than the fowls of heaven"?

C. It is Abiding and Not Transitory.

1. *Perishing pleasures.* The pleasures of sense are fading and perishing. As "the world passes away," so do the lusts of it. That which at first pleases and satisfies, after a while grows less attractive and becomes disgusting.

2. *Permanent pleasures.* The pleasures of godliness will abide; they wither not in winter, nor tarnish with time, nor does age wrinkle their beauty. Christ's joy which He gives to His own "no man takes from them."

## II. THE PROOF OF THE PLEASANTNESS OF THE GODLY LIFE.

A. The Nature of True Godliness.

1. *To know the true God and Jesus Christ.* This is the first thing we have to do to get our understandings rightly informed concerning both the object and the medium of our religious or spiritual relations.

2. *To cast all of our cares upon God.* This is to commit all our ways and works to Him with an assurance that He will care for us. To be truly godly is to have our wills melted into the will of God in everything.

3. *A life of communion with God.* Good Christians have "fellowship with the Father and with His Son, Jesus Christ" and endeavor to keep up that holy converse. In reading and meditating upon Scriptures we hear God speaking to us. In prayer and praise we speak to God.

B. The Comfort and Privileges of Godliness.

1. *The comforts purchased, promised, and provided.* Christ purchased peace and pleasure for us. What He purchased has been promised to us and provision has been made for the application of that which has been purchased and promised: the Holy Spirit, the Scriptures, the ministry.

2. *The privileges secured and procured.* They are discharged from debts of sin; they have "the Spirit of God witnessing with their spirits that they are the children of God"; they have access to the throne of grace; they have a good conscience; they have the earnests and foretastes of glory.

C. The Experience of the Godly.

1. *They find the rules and dictates of godliness agreeable and pleasant.* They have found the rules and dictates of godliness very agreeable, both to right reason and to their true interest and therefore pleasant. They have found all of God's precepts to be right and reasonable and equitable.

2. *They have found the exercise of devotion comfortable and pleasant.* If there be a heaven upon earth it is in communion with God; in hearing from Him and in speaking to Him, in receiving the tokens of His favor and communications of His grace.

3. *They find that pains and trouble are overcome by the pleasure of godliness.* For this we may appeal to the martyrs and other sufferers for the name of Christ whose spiritual joys made their bonds for Christ easy and made their prisons their delectable orchards.

4. *They find that the closer they keep to the ways of godliness the greater the pleasantness.* The more godliness prevails the greater is the pleasure. What disquiet and discomfort wisdom's children have is the result of deviation from wisdom's ways or their slothfulness and trifling in these ways.

## III. THE VINDICATION OF THE PLEASANTNESS OF THE GODLY LIFE.

A. The Misrepresentations of the Enemies of God.

1. *The manner of misrepresentation.* They suggest that Christ's yoke is heavy and His commandments grievous; to be godly is to bid adieu to all pleasure and delight and to turn tormentors to ourselves.

2. *The answer.* These enemies know not whereof they speak. Now in answer to these calumnies we have this to say that the matter is not so. Those who speak thus of godliness "speak evil of the things that they understand not."

B. **The Misrepresentation of Proposed Friends of God.**

1. *The misrepresentation stated.* Some are morose and sour in their profession — peevish and ill-humored. Others are melancholy and sorrowful in their profession, mourning under doubts and fears about their spiritual state.

2. *The reply.* (a) God is sometimes pleased for wise and holy ends, for a time, to suspend the communication of His comforts to His people. (b) It also may be the result of sin in the life. They run themselves into the dark and shut their eyes against the light.

C. **Scriptural Difficulties.**

1. *Repentance.* We must mourn for sin and reflect with regret upon our infirmities, but we must remember also that repentance is not caused by godliness; pleasure accompanies it; after repentance there is pleasure attending it.

2. *Earnest labor.* Agonizing is a part of godliness. In this there is comfort. We are enabled for it and encouraged in it.

3. *Self denial.* The sensual pleasures we are to deny are comparatively despicable and really dangerous.

4. *Tribulation.* It is but light affliction at worst and as those afflictions abound for Christ so our "consolation also aboundeth by Christ."

## CONCLUSION

Let us all then be persuaded to enter into and to walk in these paths of wisdom that are so very pleasant.

# 8

## Despising the Soul

*He that refuseth instruction despiseth his
own soul.*                    —**Proverbs 15:32**

IN THIS text Solomon in a few words gives such an
account of those whom he found he could do no good upon as
makes their folly manifest before all men. They refuse instruction
and thereby they despise their own souls.

## I. THE MANNER OF DESPISING THE SOUL.

**A. Some Despise the Soul in Opinion.** They advance notions
that subtract from the honor of the soul.

1. *Denial of the reality of the soul.* Such believe that there is
   no substance but matter and shut out all incorporeal nature.
   To them sense and perception is the product of matter and
   motion.

2. *Denial of the intelligence of the soul.* Many, in order that
   they may not be charged with neglecting salvation or incurring condemnation of their own souls, choose to despise
   them as not capable of salvation or condemnation; and that
   they may not come under the imputation of acting unreason-
   ably, ridicule reason.

3. *Denial of the immortality of the soul.* Those despise their
   own souls that deny the immortality of them; who, that
   they may justify themselves in living like beasts, expect
   no other but to die like beasts. "Let us eat and drink, for
   tomorrow we shall die" and there is an end of us.

**B. Some Despise the Soul in Practice.**

1. *They abuse the soul.* The soul is abused when it is devoted
   to the service of Satan; when it is defiled with the polutions

38

of sin; when deceived by lies and falsehoods; when distracted and disquieted with inordinate cares or griefs about this world and its things; when it has an inordinate complacency and repose in the world.

2. *They hazard the soul.* The soul is hazarded when exposed to the wrath of God by wilful sin; when we build our lives upon the sand instead of the rock; when we give them as a pawn for the gains of this world.

3. *They neglect the soul.* They despise their soul who neglect to take care of its sin-wounds, who fail to get the wants of the soul supplied, who fail to guard their soul, who neglect the soul's eternal welfare.

4. *They consider the body more important than the soul.* Such employ the soul only to serve their bodies, whereas the body was made to serve the soul. They injure the soul to please the body. They endanger the soul to please the body.

## II. THE FOLLY OF DESPISING THE SOUL.

### A. This is Seen When We Consider the Nature of the Soul.

1. *It is of divine origin.* The soul of man is of divine origin; it was not made of dust as the body was, but it was the breath of the Almighty. It had the image of God stamped upon it and is the masterpiece of God's workmanship on the earth.

2. *It can know God.* It is capable of knowing God and conversing with Him; it is capable of being sanctified by the spirit and grace of God; it is capable of being glorified with God, of seeing Him as He is.

3. *It is capable of self-consciousness.* Self-consciousness is in the nature of the soul. The soul is capable of reflecting upon itself and conversing with itself.

### B. This is Seen When We Consider the Nearness of the Soul.

1. *It is man's possession.* Our soul is our own, for we are entrusted with it as committed to our charge by God to be

employed in His service now and fitted for a happiness hereafter.

2. *It is the man himself.* The soul is the man, and what is the man but a living soul? Abstract the soul as living and the body is a lump of clay; abstract the soul as rational and the man is as the beasts that perish.

C. **This is Seen When We Consider the Purchase of the Soul.**

1. *It was not purchased by silver and gold.* As silver and gold would not satisfy the desires of a soul nor its capacities, so neither would they satisfy for the sins of the soul. We are "not redeemed with corruptible things."

2. *It was purchased by the blood of Christ.* Christ gave Himself, His own precious blood to be a ransom for our souls, a counter-price. He made His soul an offering for ours. Nothing less would buy them back out of the hands of Divine Justice — would save them from ruin and secure to them their blessedness.

D. **This is Seen When We Consider the Projects concerning the Soul.** The Holy Spirit is striving with men's souls to sanctify and save them; the evil spirit goes about continually seeking to debauch and destroy them.

1. *The projects of God.* Think what projects the love of God has to save souls. He sent His Son to seek and save lost souls. He has given His Spirit to work upon our spirits and to witness to them. He has appointed ministers of the gospel to "watch for your souls."

2. *The projects of Satan.* Think also what projects Satan has to ruin souls. What devices, what depths, what wiles he has in hunting for precious souls and how all the forces of the powers of darkness are kept continually in arms to war against the soul.

E. **This is Seen When We Consider the Perpetual Duration of the Soul.**

1. *The fact of its perpetual duration.* The soul is an immortal spirit that will last and live forever. The spirit of a man

is that candle of the Lord which will never be blown out
or burnt out.

2. *The place of the perpetual duration of the soul.* The soul
will not only live and act when separated from the body,
but it must be somewhere forever. There is everlasting
happiness or everlasting misery designed for souls in the
other world, according to their character in this and according as they are found at death.

## CONCLUSION

Let us see and bewail our folly in having such low thoughts of
our souls and learn to put due value upon them. Let us value
other things as they have relation to our souls. Let us not despise
the souls of others and in love do all we can for their salvation.

# 9

## The Folly of Despising our own Ways

*But he that despiseth his ways shall die.*
*—Proverbs 19:16*

W E HAVE here fair warning to a careless world. O that it were taken! There are those by whom it is taken. David speaks of it with comfort that he had taken the alarms which God's commands gave and therefore hoped for the rewards they proposed (Psalm 19:11).

### I. THE SINNER'S FALL AND RUIN: "he shall die."

### A. It is a Spiritual Death.

1. *The soul destitute of spiritual life.* An impenitent soul lies under the wrath and curse of God which is its death. It is destitute of spiritual life and of its principles and powers. It is under the dominion of corruption which is as killing to the soul as the curse of God is a killing sentence.

2. *The soul separated from communion with God.* They shall die; that is, they shall be cut off from all communion with God, which is the life of the soul, and from all hope of His loving kindness, which is better than life. They shall die; that is, they shall be dead to God and to all good.

### B. It is an Eternal Death. The eternal or second death is the sinfulness of man and the wrath of God immutably fixed. It is not the extinguishing of men's beings, but the extinguishing of their bliss.

1. *It is real.* Misery and torment in the next world will certainly be the portion of all who live and die ungodly (Romans 2:5-11).

42

2. *It is fearful.* The second death is inconceivably dreadful. Who knows what is the power of God's anger, either what He can inflict or what it is possible for a soul to suffer — or what a fearful thing it is for a sinner that has made himself obnoxious to God's justice?

3. *It is near.* There is but a step between the sinner and the second death and it may be a stort step and soon taken. There is only one life between the sinner and hell and that is the sinner's own life which may shortly come to an end.

## II. THE SINNER'S FAULT AND FOLLY: "despiseth his ways."

### A. The Meaning of Despising our own Ways.

1. *Unconcern about the end of our ways.* This includes: (a) Failure to consider and direct our ways toward the God-purposed aim or end of our lives, namely, to show forth the praise of God and to live for Christ. (b) Failure to enquire what will be the last end in which our ways will terminate — heaven or hell.

2. *Indifference to the rule of our ways.* We despise our way if we set aside the rules which God has given us to obey: the Scriptures; and conscience in subordination to the Bible. We despise our way if we set up our rules of life in opposition to God's. Such are guided by personal desires and the cause and custom of this world.

3. *Wavering in the course of our ways.* It is certain those have not the concern they ought to have who have not resolution enough to persist in good purposes and to hold to them and have not sufficient constancy to proceed and persevere in the good practices wherein they have begun.

4. *Failure to acknowledge and apply ourselves to God.* This honor God has been pleased to put upon our ways, that He has undertaken to be our guide and guard in them, if we look up to Him as we ought (Psalms 37:23; 73:24; Isaiah 40:31); if therefore we do not have our eyes upon Him, if we make light of this privilege, as all those do who do not make use of it, we lose this honor.

5. *Careless of our past ways.* It is our concern to look back, because if we have done amiss there is a way provided to undo it by repentance. If we are unwilling that others should reprove us for wrong or to examine and correct ourselves we despise our own ways.

6. *Heedless and inconsiderate of the way before us.* If we think that God is neither pleased nor displeased with our thoughts, affections, words, or actions; if we do not care to avoid sin and do our duty as it ought to be done, we are careless of our way and despise it.

B. **The Foolishness and Danger of Despising our own Ways.**

1. *God observes our ways.* The God of heaven observes and takes particular notice of all our ways, even the ways of our hearts — their thoughts and intents are open before His eyes (Hebrews 4:13). He sees our ways as things that must be judged and which judgment must be given justly.

2. *Satan seeks to pervert our ways.* Satan is a subtle enemy that seeks to pervert our ways and to draw us into his service and interests. Satan's design is more than half accomplished when he has brought men to a state of indifference as to their actions and they let things go just as they will.

3. *Many persons watch us.* David prayed, "Lord, lead me in a plain path because of mine enemies" — because of them that observe me (Psalm 27:11). There are many who take notice of what we do and say: some watch us as a pattern; others, to reproach; still others, to rejoice when we walk in the truth.

4. *Man must give an account of all his ways.* As there is now an account kept of all sins in the book of God's omniscience and of the sinner's own conscience, so there must shortly be an account given of them all. They must all be reviewed. It is a folly for us to despise our own ways and make a light matter of them.

THE FOLLY OF DESPISING OUR OWN WAYS       45

5. *Our ways most likely will determine our future life.* As you spend your time you are likely to spend your eternity. If the prevailing temper of your mind now is vain, carnal, selfish, sensual, earthly, and worldly, and you go out of the world under the dominion of such a temper you are utterly unfit for heaven and so is heaven for you.

## CONCLUSION

Are you in the broad way that leads to destruction, or in the narrow way that leads to life; among the many who walk in the way of their own hearts or among the few that walk in the way of God's commandments?   Christ is the way — are you in the Christ?

# 10

# A Worthy Tribute to a Godly Mother

> *Her children shall rise up, and call her blessed.*
> —Proverbs 31:28

THIS is part of the just debt owing to the virtuous woman that answers the characters laid down in the foregoing verses; and part of the reward promised and secured to her by Him who in both worlds is and will be "the Rewarder of them that diligently seek and serve Him."

## I. THE CHARACTER OF THE MOTHER DESERVING THE TRIBUTE.

### A. She is Wise and Kind (verse 26).

1. *The effects of her wisdom.* Wisdom dictates her conversation. By opening the mouth with wisdom there is instilled in children's minds what they will afterwards have use. Such children will have reason to call their mother blessed for setting them an example for the good government of a tongue.

2. *The description of her kindness.* She is truly kind, that is, wisely so; she is tender to her children's comfort, but not indulgent of her children's follies. The mother who has this law in her tongue and in her heart and is always under its commands and regulations gains her children's love and is entitled to their good word.

### B. She is Industrious (verse 27).

1. *She is concerned for her family.* She takes care of her family and all the affairs of it. She does not intermeddle in the concerns of other people's houses, she thinks it enough for her to look well to her own.

2. *She is a good home-maker.* Most of the characteristics given to her in the verses preceding the text fall under this head, where she is commended for her diligence and consideration in the management of her house and the affairs of it, which is her particular calling. It is to her praise that she looks well to the ways of her household, appointing them their portion of food and work.

## C. She is Virtuous (verse 29).

1. *The meaning of virtue.* Virtue is vigor and boldness and resolution in that which is good; courage and spirit in doing our duty, in facing difficulties, giving reproofs, bearing reproaches, in proving opportunities, and pressing forward towards perfection. They are lively and cheerful, fervent in spirit, serving the Lord.

2. *The excellency of virtue.* Many daughters in their father's house, and in their single state, have done virtuously, but a good wife and mother, if she is virtuous, excels them all and does more good in her place than they can do in theirs. A man cannot have his house so well kept by good daughters as by a good wife and mother.

## D. She is Godly.

1. *The importance of piety.* It is the fear of God that crowns the character of this virtuous woman, without which, all the rest is of small account. She does not lack that "one thing needful." In all that she does she is guided and governed by the principles of conscience and a regard to God.

2. *The description of piety.* It is a holy awe and reverence of God that sets Him always before us, recognizing His authority and submitting ourselves to His precepts and His providence. It glorifies God as the greatest and best of beings and evidences it in a steady, uniform, and unhypocritical devotion.

## II. THE CHILDREN'S DUTY IN RELATION TO A GODLY MOTHER.

## A. Grateful Remembrance.

1. *Of physical care.* The tender and earnest care which God placed in the hearts of our mothers when we were in the

helpless state of innocency, the pains they took with us when we were unable to do anything for ourselves, for all of this we can never make sufficient return.

2. *Of spiritual nurture.*  As godly mothers we ought to do honor to their names and their memory should be doubly precious to us, remembering that under God we "owe unto them our own souls." Blessed are they of the Lord who taught us the knowledge of the Lord Jesus and followed it with constant and earnest prayers.

## B. Fervent Thanksgiving.

1. *For God's grace in them.*  The grace which led them on in their way and bore them as "upon eagles' wings," until He had brought them safely and comfortably to their journey's end — to that blessed state where they receive the end of their faith and hope, even the completion of the salvation of their souls.

2. *For our benefit by the grace in them.*  Although they could not give us grace, yet God was pleased to make use of them as instruments in His hand in the beginning and carrying on of that good work. God enabled them to be guides to us and faithful monitors.

## C. Acknowledge the Goodness of their Way.

1. *They were honorable.*  We must reckon that they were truly honorable and place more value on the fact that we are all children of saints rather than the children of nobles. This will quicken us to pursue honor in the same way in which "they attained a good report." Let us then have the same honor that our godly mothers had.

2. *They were happy.*  They were happy in the enjoyment of themselves and of what God had given them in this world; happy in the quiet and repose of their own minds; and happy in the prospect of better things in the better country. The ways of God and godliness are good ways.

## D. Follow in their Steps of Virtue and Piety.

1. *In compliance with their example.*  We ought to imitate them in everything that was praiseworthy. In compliance

to the good example they set us, and in conformity to that, by which the instructions they gave us were both explained and enforced, and we were directed and encouraged in the way of duty.

2. *In expectation of the bliss of heaven.* Their serious piety was found unto praise and honor and glory in this world and will be much more so at the appearing of Jesus Christ. Let us therefore, having an eye to the same joy, run with patience the same race set before us. Let us proceed with holy vigor and persevere with an unshaken constancy.

## CONCLUSION

It is, indeed, enough to make them truly and eternally happy that virtuous people are blessed of God; and "those whom He blesseth they are blessed indeed"; His pronouncing them happy makes them so. This is enough to engage us all to, and encourage us all in, the study and practice of virtue and piety.

# 11

## Surrender to God's Call

> *Also I heard the voice of the Lord, saying,*
> *Whom shall I send, and who will go for*
> *us? Then said I, Here am I; send me.*
> —Isaiah 6:8

PERHAPS of all the Old Testament prophets, none had a more awful and solemn mission than the prophet Isaiah; who spoke so plainly and fully of Christ and the grace of the gospel. If we look back to the preparation for his call (Isaiah 6:5-6) we shall see the prophet deeply touched by a humbling sense of his own sinfulness and a comfortable sense of his acceptance with God. The prophet being thus prepared has the work and trust committed to him.

### I. THE COUNSEL OF GOD CONCERNING ISAIAH'S MISSION.

Although God needs not to be counselled by others nor to consult with Himself, yet sometimes the wisdom of God, though never at a loss, is expressed by a solemn consultation, to show that what God does is the result of an eternal counsel.

### A. The Consultants.

1. *God in His glory.* It is God in His glory, the same that Isaiah saw in the first verse, *upon His throne, high and lifted up.* Not that he saw God's essence, no man has seen that or can see it, but such a display of His glory in vision, as He was pleased at this time to manifest Himself by, as to Moses and Israel at Mount Sinai.

2. *God in three persons.* This is plainly intimated in the plural number, *us.* It is one God who says, "Whom shall I send" and yet this One is three persons, the very same who said

"Let *us* make man." To throw more light upon and to add greater weight, it is observable that the words which follow in the next two verses (Isaiah 6:9-10) are in the New Testament applied both to the Son (John 12:40) and to the Holy Spirit (Acts 28:25-26).

### B. The Consultation.

1. *The content of the consultation.* "Whom shall I send and who will go for us." This refers to all the messages which Isaiah was intrusted to deliver in God's name. Not that God was in doubt as to whom to send; when He has a work to do, He will not want instruments to do it by, for He can find men fit or make them so; but it intimates that the business was such as required a well accomplished messenger beyond those whom He had hitherto employed.

2. *Observations of the consultation.* Now we may gather three observations: (a) It is the unspeakable favor of God to us that He is pleased to communicate His mind to us and to make it known by men like ourselves. (b) It is a rare thing to find one who is fit to go for God, to carry His messages to the children of men. (c) None are allowed to go for God but those who are sent by Him.

## II. THE CONSENT OF ISAIAH TO HIS GOD-GIVEN MISSION.

The errand on which Isaiah was to go was a very melancholy errand, yet he offered himself to the service. When we are called to act or speak for God we must go and leave the success to Him.

### A. His Readiness.

1. *A response without objections.* Isaiah does not make objections as Moses did when he said, "O my Lord, I am not eloquent" (Exodus 4:10), or "Send by the hand of him whom Thou wilt send" (Exodus 4:13), anybody but me; but he responds, "Behold me; I present myself to Thee to be employed as Thou pleasest."

2. *A voluntary response.* He was a volunteer in the service; not pressed into it, but willing in this day of power. In this as in other things God loves a cheerful giver, a cheerful offerer. In all acts of obedience to the calls of God and assistance to the work of God we must be free and forward as those who know that we serve a good Master and His work is honorable and glorious.

## B. His Resolution.

1. *It is firm and fixed.* The prophet gives not only a free consent; but he is firm and fixed in it; he does not hesitate or waver, but is ready both to swear by it and to perform it; and he will not be beaten off it no more than the people of Israel, when they said, "Nay, but we will serve the Lord" (Joshua 24:21); or Ruth, when she said, "Entreat me not to leave thee, or to turn from following after thee" (Ruth 1:16).

2. *It is to abide by the service to the end, even through great difficulties.* Here am I, not only ready to go, but resolved in the strength of divine grace to encounter the greatest difficulties and to abide by the service to the end. Send me and I will adhere to it whatever it cost me and will never draw back. And good reason have we thus to serve Christ for with such a steady and unshaken resolution did He undertake to save us. Those who thus set out with resolution may depend upon God to bear them out.

## C. His Referring Himself to God.
His expressing himself thus, "Here am I, send me," intimates this: Lord, employ me as Thou thinkest fit; cut out what work thou pleasest for me. I will never prescribe, but ever subscribe. Here am I, ready to go to whom and on what errand Thou wilt, whatever objections may be made against it. Lord, I am at Thy service, entirely at Thy disposal. Let the will of God be done by me and done concerning me.

1. *To have God's will done by him.*

2. *To have God's will done concerning him.*

## CONCLUSION

We must go forth in the strength of the Lord God or we shall go to no purpose.  If we think to succeed in our strength, by our own wisdom or importunity, we only deceive ourselves.  If, when God calls to you to appear and act for Him, you cheerfully say, "Here am I," you may be sure when you call to Him, He will also say, "Here am I."  If you say, "Lord, send me," He will say, "Go, and I will be with thee."

# 12

## Christ the Suffering Substitute

*All we, like sheep, have gone astray; we
have turned every one to his own way;
and the Lord hath laid on Him the iniquity of us all.* —Isaiah 53:6

It WAS a great mystery that so excellent a person
should suffer such hard things; and it was natural to ask, "How
did it come about? What evil did He do?" His enemies looked
upon Him as suffering justly for His crimes; and though they
could lay nothing to His charge they considered Him smitten of
God. Because they hated Him and persecuted him, they thought
that God did likewise and that He was His enemy and fought
against Him. They that saw Him hanging on the cross enquired
not into the merits of His cause, but took it for granted that He
was guilty of everything laid to His charge and that therefore
vengeance suffered Him not to live. It is true, He was smitten of
God, but not in the sense in which they meant it. It was for our
good and in our stead.

## I. MAN'S GUILT.

A. **The Extent of it.** It is certain that we are all guilty before
God; we have all sinned and have come short of the glory of
God (Romans 3:23). "All we like sheep have gone astray,"
one as well as another; the whole race of mankind lies under
the stain of original corruption and every individual stands
charged with many actual transgressions. We have all gone
astray from God our rightful Owner, alienated ourselves from
Him, from the ends He designed us to move towards and the
way He appointed us to move in.

B. **The Nature of it.** We have gone astray like sheep which
are apt to wander and are unapt, when they have gone astray,

54

to find the way home again. That is our true character; we are bent to wander from God, but altogether unable of ourselves to return to Him. This is mentioned not only as our infelicity (that we go astray from the green pastures and expose ourselves to the beasts of prey), but as our iniquity. Sinners have their own iniquity, their beloved sin, which does most easily beset them; their own evil way of which they are particularly fond.

1. *It is a wandering from God.*

2. *It is iniquity.*[1]

C. **The Seriousness of it.** We affront God in going astray from Him, for we turn aside every one to his own way and thereby set up ourselves and our own will in competition with God and His will; which is the malignity of sin. Instead of walking obediently in God's way we have turned wilfully and stubbornly to our own way, the way of our own heart, the way in which our own corrupt appetites and passions lead us. We have set up for ourselves to be our own masters, our own carvers, to do what we will and to have what we will.

1. *We insult God.*

2. *We are wilfully disobedient to God.*

## II. GOD'S PROVISION.

A. **The Appointment of Christ by the Will of the Father.** Our Lord Jesus was appointed to make satisfaction for our sins and to save us from the penal consequences of them by the will of His Father, for "the Lord hath laid on Him the iniquity of us all." God chose Him to be the Savior of poor sinners and would have Him to save them in this way, by bearing their sins and the punishment of them; not the same that we should have suffered, but that which was more than equivalent for the maintaining of the honor of the holiness and justice of God in the government of the world. Christ was delivered to death by the determinate counsel and foreknowledge of God (Acts 2:23). None but God had the power to lay

---

1. More literally, transgression—Ed.

our sins upon Christ because the sin was committed against Him and to Him the satisfaction was to be made and because Christ, His own Son, was sinless.

1. *He was appointed to make satisfaction for sins.*

2. *He was appointed to save men from the penal consequences of sin.*

B. **The Transference of our sins upon Christ.** The way we are saved from the ruin of sin is by the laying of our sins on Christ as the sins of the Old Testament offerer were laid upon the sacrifice. Our sins were made to meet or fall upon Him. The laying of our sins upon Christ implies the taking of them off from us. We shall not fall under the curse of the law if we submit to the grace of the Gospel. They were laid upon Christ when He was made sin, a sin-offering, for us and redeemed us from the curse of the law by being made a curse for us.

1. *The fact of the transference of our sins upon Christ illustrated in the Old Testament.*

2. *The implication of the transference of our sins upon Christ.*

C. **The Extent of the Atonement.** It was the iniquity of us all that was laid on Christ; for in Him there is a sufficiency of merit for the salvation of all, which excludes none that do not exclude themselves. It intimates that this is the one only way of salvation. All that are justified are justified by having their sins laid on Jesus Christ and though they were ever so many, He is able to bear the weight of them all.

1. *It is sufficient for all.*

2. *It is efficient only to those who believe.*

## CONCLUSION

God laid upon Christ our iniquity; but did He consent to it? Yes, He did. Therefore, when He was seized He requested those into whose hands He surrendered Himself that His surrender should be His disciples' discharge: "If ye seek me, let those go their way" (John 18:8). By His own voluntary will He made Himself responsible for our debt. Because He did the Father's will and made atonement for the sin of man He rolled away the reproach of His death and stamped immortal honor upon His sufferings notwithstanding the disgrace and ignominy of them.

# 13

## A Gracious Invitation

> *Ho, everyone that thirsteth, come ye to the waters, and he that hath no money; come ye, buy and eat; yea, come, buy wine and milk without money, and without price.*
>
> —Isaiah 55:1

W E ARE invited to come and take the benefit of that provision which the grace of God has made for souls, of that which is "the heritage of the servants of the Lord" (Isaiah 54:17) and not only their heritage hereafter, but their cup now.

## I. THE PERSONS INVITED.

### A. The Extent of the Invitation.

1. *The fact.* Jews and Gentiles. "Ho (take notice of it; he that hath ears to hear, let him hear), every one." Not the Jews only, to whom first the word of salvation was sent, but the Gentiles, the poor and the maimed, the halt and the blind, are called to this marriage supper, whoever can be picked up out of the highways and the hedges.

2. *The intimation.* Christ is sufficient for all. It intimates that in Christ there is enough for all and enough for each; that ministers are to make a general offer of life and salvation to all; that in gospel times the invitation should be more largely made than it had been, and should be sent to the Gentiles.

### B. The Qualification for Acceptance of the Invitation.

1. *Desire is necessary.* They must thirst. All are welcome to gospel grace only upon these terms, that gospel grace is welcome to them. Those who are satisfied with the

world and its enjoyments; those who depend upon the
merit of their own works for righteousness; these do not
thirst, they have no sense of need and therefore they will
not condescend to behold Christ. Those who thirst are
invited to waters as those who labor and are heavy laden
are invited to Christ for rest.

2. *Desire must precede the gift of grace.* Where God gives
grace, He first gives to thirst after it; and where He has
given to thirst after it, He will give it.

## II. THE RESPONSIBILITY OF THE PERSONS IN-VITED.

### A. They are to Come to the Waters.

1. *It is the place of supply.* Come to the water-side, to the
ports, and queys, and wharfs, on the navigable rivers into
which goods are imported, thither come and buy, for that is
the marketplace of foreign commodities; and to us they
would have been forever foreign, if Christ had not brought
in an everlasting righteousness.

2. *It is a picture of coming to Christ our Savior.* Come to
Christ for He is the Fountain opened, He is the smitten
Rock. Come to the healing waters, come to the living
waters; "whosoever will let him take of the water of life"
(Revelation 22:17). Our Savior referred to it when He
said, "If any man thirst, let him come unto me and drink"
(John 7:37).

### B. They are to Come and Partake.

1. *They are to come and buy.* Come and buy, and we can
assure you that you shall have a good bargain of which
you will never repent nor lose by it. Come and buy; make
it your own by an application of the grace of the Gospel
to yourselves; make it your own upon Christ's terms and
stand not hesitating about the terms or deliberating whether
you shall agree to them.

2. *They are to come and eat.* Make it still more your own,
as that which we eat is more our own than that which we

only buy. We must buy the truth, not that we may lay it by to be looked at, but that we may feed and feast upon it and that the spiritual life may be nourished and strengthened by it. When we have bought what we need let us not deny ourselves the comfortable use of it.

## III. THE PROVISION OF THE INVITATION.

### A. The Substance of the Provision.

1. *The substance stated.* "Come and buy wine and milk," which will not only quench the thirst, but nourish the body and revive the spirits. The world comes short of our expectations; we promise ourselves, at least, water in it, but we are disappointed of that. But Christ out-does our expectations; we come to the waters and would be glad of them, but we find there wine and milk.

2. *The truth taught.* We must come to Christ to have milk for babes, to nourish and cherish them that are but lately born again; and with Him strong men shall find that which will be a cordial to them; they shall have wine to make glad their hearts. We must part with our poison that we may procure this wine and milk.

### B. The Communication of the Provision.

1. *The freeness of the offer.* "Buy wine and milk without money, and without price." A strange way of buying, not only without ready money (that is common enough), but without any money or the promise of any; yet it seems not so strange to those who have observed Christ's counsel to the Laodicean Church that was wretchedly poor, "and knowest not that thou art wretched, and miserable, and poor, and blind, and naked: I counsel thee to buy of me gold tried in the fire, that thou mayest be rich" (Revelation 3:17-18).

2. *The implications of the freeness of the offer.* Our buying without money intimates: (a) that the gifts offered are invaluable. (b) He makes these proposals, not because He has occasion to sell, but because He has a disposition to

give. (c) The things offered are already bought and payment made.    Christ paid the price of purchase.    (d) We
are welcome to the benefits of the promise, though we are
utterly unworthy of them and unable to purchase them.

## CONCLUSION

We ourselves are not of any value, nor anything that we have
or can do, and we must own it, that if Christ and heaven be ours
we must see ourselves forever indebted to free grace.    "For by
grace are ye saved through faith; and that not of yourselves: it
is the gift of God: not of works, lest any man should boast"
(Ephesians 2:8, 9).

## 14

# The Year of the Redeemed

*The year of my redeemed is come.*

*—Isaiah 63:4*

THERE will come a year of redemption for those who suffer in the cause of Christ. God will not and men shall not contend forever; nor shall the rod of the wicked rest always upon the lot of the righteous, although it may rest long there.

## I. THE DESCRIPTION OF THE YEAR OF THE REDEEMED.

### A. The Year of Recompence for the Controversy of Zion (Isaiah 34:8).

1. *For the sons of Zion.* God espouses the cause of the sons of Zion who have been abused by their enemies and trodden down and broken to pieces as earthen pitchers.

2. *For the worship of Zion.* Jehovah's controversy is for the songs of Zion which their persecutors have profaned by their insolence and contempt of the Jews and their religion when they upbraided them in their captivity with the songs of Zion (Psalm 137:3, 8).

3. *For the powers of the king of Zion* which the enemies have usurped. The offices of our Lord have been invaded by corrupt ecclesiasticism. Shall not the crown of the exalted Redeemer be supported against these usurpations?

4. *For the pleasant things of the palaces of Zion* which have been laid waste. God keeps an account of the mischief done at any time and will bring it all into the reckoning when the year of recompences comes.

## B. The Year of Release for God's Captives.

1. *Release from oppressed consciences.* The compliance to
tyranny while the soul remains unbended is a grievous
affliction; the freeing of the oppressed from this force will
be a most glorious deliverance.

2. *Release of oppressed confessors.* Humanity obliges us much
and Christianity much more, to pity the distressed state of
those who are in bonds and banishment for the Word of
God and for the testimony of Jesus Christ. Then shall be
the time when the house of the prisoners shall be opened
and every man's chains fall from his hands.

## C. The Year of the Revival of Primitive Christianity.

1. *Prominence of godliness among men.* The year of the re-
vival of primitive Christianity in the power of it will be
the year of the redeemed. This we long to see, the domi-
nance of serious godliness in the lives of all who are called
Christians.

2. *World-wide spread of the Gospel.* When the bounds of
Christianity will be enlarged by the conversion of nations to
the faith of Christ; when the kingdoms of this world become
the kingdoms of the Lord and His Christ and the Redeemer's throne set up where Satan's seat is, then will the
year of the Redeemed come.

3. *Suppression of sin.* Mistakes shall be rectified, corruptions
purged out. Every plant that is not of our heavenly Father's
planting shall be rooted up and the plants that are of His
planting shall be fruitful and flourishing. Vice and profan-
ity shall be suppressed and all iniquity shall stop her mouth.

4. *Unity among God's people.* Divisions shall be healed and
the unity of the Spirit kept in the bond of peace. All shall
agree to love one another although they cannot agree in
everything to think with one another.

5. *Outpouring of the Holy Spirit.* The Spirit shall be poured
out from on high so that truth will triumph over error, devotion over profaneness, virtue over all immoralities, justice
and truth over treachery and all unrighteousness.

## II. THE GROUND FOR THE CERTAINTY OF THE COMING OF THE YEAR OF THE REDEEMED.

### A. The Justice and Righteousness of God.

1. *The fact of God's justice and righteousness.* Though clouds and darkness are round about God so that we know not the way that He takes, yet judgment and justice are the habitation of His throne; and so will it appear when the mystery of God shall be finished and the heavens shall declare His righteousness.

2. *The encouragement of God's justice and righteousness.* Look up with an eye of faith to heaven above and see the Lord God Omnipotent upon a throne, high and lifted up; the throne of glory, the throne of government which He has prepared and established in the heavens.

3. *The certainty of God's just and righteous acts.* They are mistaken who think that God has forsaken the earth; who say in their hearts: "God hath forgotten" and "will not require it" (Psalm 10:11, 13). The day is coming when it shall be evident and every man will own it. "Verily there is a reward for the righteous: verily there is a God that judgeth the earth" (Psalm 58:11).

### B. The Performance of God's Promises to His People in All Ages.

1. *This is evidenced in the history of the Jewish nation.* God came to deliver Israel from Egyptian bondage. In the times of the judges first one enemy and then another oppressed them, but in due time God raised up deliverers. The Babylonian captivity came to an end.

2. *This is evidenced in the history of the Christian church.* The Christian church has been often afflicted. Many have been the troubles of the followers of Christ, but the Lord has delivered them out of them all.

## III. THE ENCOURAGEMENT TO HOPE FOR THE APPROACHING OF THE YEAR OF THE REDEEMED.

### A. The Measure of Iniquity is Increasing. The measure of the iniquity of the church's enemies fills apace. The powers

with which we are contesting seem to grow more and more false and treacherous, cruel, and barbarous; which cannot but ripen their vintage for the great wine-press of the wrath of God (Revelation 14:19).

B. **The Present Shaping of Affairs Presents a Hopeful Prospect.** As for God, His work is perfect; when He begins He will make an end. What we have received from God emboldens us to expect more.

## IV. THE CHRISTIAN'S DUTY IN REFERENCE TO THE YEAR OF THE REDEEMED.

A. **It is His Duty to Engage in Earnest Prayer.** When Daniel understood by books that the seventy years of Jerusalem's desolations were expiring he set his face to seek the Lord by prayer and supplication, with fasting. When we see mercies coming toward us let us meet them by our prayers.

B. **It is His Duty to be Obedient to the Laws of Love and Holiness.** Let us prepare ourselves by bringing every thought into obedience to the two royal laws of holiness and love. When we expect God to do wonders among us, it concerns us to sanctify ourselves.

C. **It is His Duty to Patiently Wait for the Year of the Redeemed.** If the days of our brethren's afflictions should be prolonged and their deliverance be deferred, yet let us not be weary, nor faint in our minds. The year of the redeemed will come at the time infinite Wisdom has appointed.

## CONCLUSION

Let us give all diligence to make sure our eternal redemption and then we shall be happy, though we live not to see the glories of the year of the redeemed on earth.

# 15

## A Glorious Description of God

> God is jealous, and the Lord revengeth;
> the Lord revengeth, and is furious: the
> Lord will take vengeance on His adversar-
> ies, and He reserveth wrath for His ene-
> mies. The Lord is slow to anger, and great
> in power, and will not at all acquit.
> —Nahum 1:2-3

NINEVEH knows not God, that God which contends with her, and therefore is here told what a God He is. It is good for us all to mix faith with that which is here said concerning Him, which speaks a great deal of terror to the wicked and comfort to good people. This glorious description of the Sovereign of the world, like the pillar of cloud and fire, has a bright side towards Israel and a dark side toward the Egyptians.

## I. HE IS A GOD OF INFLEXIBLE JUSTICE.

### A. He Resents the Insults and Indignities of Men.

1. *The breadth of His jealousy.* He resents the affronts and indignities done Him by those who deny His being or any of His perfections, that set up other gods in competition with Him, that destroy His laws, or ridicule His Word. He is jealous for His own honor in the matters of His worship and will not endure a rival; He is jealous for the comfort of His worshippers; He is jealous for His land and will not have that injured.

2. *The nature of His fury.* God is a revenger and He is furious; He has fury (so the word is), not as man has it, in whom it is an ungoverned passion, but He has it in such a way as becomes the righteous God. He has anger,

66

but He has it at command and under government. He is always Lord of His anger.

## B. He Reckons with the Men who Insult Him.

1. *The certainty of it.* We are not only told that God is a Revenger, but that He will take vengeance. Whoever are His adversaries and enemies among men, He will make them feel His resentments; and though the sentence against His enemies is not executed speedily, yet He reserves wrath for them and reserves them for it in the day of wrath.

2. *An illustration of it.* This revelation of the wrath of God against His enemies is applied to Nineveh (verse 8). The army of the Chaldeans shall overrun the country of the Assyrians and lay it all waste. "Darkness shall pursue His enemies," terror and trouble shall follow them whithersoever they go. If they think to flee from the darkness they will fall into that which is before them.

## II. HE IS A GOD OF IRRESISTIBLE POWER.

### A. The Power of God Asserted and Proved.

1. *The testimony of the atmospheric heaven.* If we look up into the regions of the air we shall find proofs of God's power. He has "His way in the whirlwind and in the storm" (verse 3). Wherever there is a whirlwind and a storm God has the command of it, the control of it, makes His way through it, goes His way in it, and serves His own purpose by it.

2. *The testimony of the deep.* If we cast our eye upon the great deeps we find that the sea is His; He made it and when He pleases He rebukes it and makes it dry. He gave proofs of His power when He divided the Red Sea and the Jordan River (Exodus 14:21-22; Joshua 3:13; 4:10, 11, 19).

3. *The testimony of the earth.* If we look around us on this earth we find proofs of His power. His power is often seen in earthquakes which shake the mountains and melt the hills. When He pleases "the earth is burnt at His presence by the scorching heat of the sun" (verse 5).

B. The Power of God in Relation to His Anger.

1. *God is a consuming fire.* If God is an almighty God we may thence infer, "Who can stand before His indignation?" (verse 6). See God here as "a consuming fire" (Hebrews 13:29), terrible and mighty. Here is His indignation against sin, His fury poured out, not like water, but like fire, like the fire and brimstone rained upon Sodom (Psalm 11:6).

2. *Sinners are an unequal match for the wrath of God.* "Who can abide in the fierceness of His anger?" (verse 6). As it is irresistible, so it is intolerable. Some of the effects of God's displeasure in this world a man may bear up under, but the fierceness of His anger, when it fastens immediately upon the soul, who can bear it?

## III. HE IS A GOD OF INFINITE MERCY

A. This is Seen in that He is Slow to Anger.

He is not easily provoked, but ready to show mercy to those who have offended Him and to receive them into favor upon their repentance.

1. *He is not easily provoked.*

2. *He is ready to show mercy.*

B. This is Seen in that He Cares for His Own.

1. *God is good to those who trust Him.* When the tokens of His rage against the wicked are abroad, He takes care for the safety and comfort of His own people (verse 7). The Lord is good to those who are good and to them He will be "a stronghold in the day of trouble."

2. *God's power is employed for the protection and satisfaction of His children.* The same almighty power that is exerted for the terror and destruction of the wicked is engaged and shall be employed for the protection and satisfaction of His own people. He is able both to save and to destroy. In the day of public trouble, when God's judgments are in the earth, He will be a place of defence to those that by faith put themselves under His protection, those that trust in

Him in the way of their duty, that live a life of dependence upon Him and devotedness to Him.

## CONCLUSION

Let each one take his portion from this passage of Scripture. Let sinners read it and tremble; let saints read it and triumph. The wrath of God is here revealed from heaven against His enemies, His favor and mercy are here assured to His faithful, loyal subjects and in both is revealed His almighty power, making His wrath very terrible and His favor very desirable.

# 16

## God's Gracious Notice of His Saints

> *Then they that feared the Lord spake often one to another; and the Lord hearkened, and heard it, and a book of remembrance was written before Him for them that feared the Lord, and that thought upon His name. And they shall be mine, saith the Lord of Hosts, in that day when I make up my jewels; and I will spare them, as a man spareth his own son that serveth him.*
> —Malachi 3:16-17

HERE IS the gracious notice God takes of the pious talk of the saints and the gracious recompence of it. Even in this corrupt and degenerate age, when there was so great a decay, nay, so great a contempt of serious godliness, there were some that retained their integrity and zeal for God.

## I. THE MANNER IN WHICH THE SAINTS DISTINGUISHED THEMSELVES.

### A. They Feared the Lord.

1. *They reverenced God.* This fear of the Lord is the beginning of wisdom (Psalm 111:10) and the root of all godliness. They reverenced the majesty of God, submitted to His authority, and had a dread of His wrath in all that they thought and said.

2. *They complied with God.* They humbly complied with God and never spake any stout words against Him as was commonly done in Malachi's day (verse 13). In every age there has been a remnant that feared the Lord, though sometimes but a little remnant.

## B. They Thought upon the Lord's Name.

1. *They meditated upon God.* They seriously considered and frequently meditated upon the discoveries God has made of Himself in His Word and by His providences; and their meditation of Him was sweet to them and influenced them.

2. *They desired to honor God.* They consulted the honor of God and aimed at that as their ultimate end in all they did. Those that know the name of God should often think of and dwell upon it in their thoughts. It is a copious, curious subject and frequent thoughts of it will contribute much to our communion with God and the stirring up of our devout affections to Him.

## C. They Spoke Often of God.

1. *The nature of their conversation.* They spoke often one to another concerning the God they feared and that name of His of which they thought so much; for out of the abundance of the heart the mouth will speak; and a good man out of the good treasure of these will bring forth good things (Luke 6:45).

2. *The purpose of their conversation.* They that feared the Lord kept together as those that were company for each other. They spoke kindly and endearingly one to another for the preserving and promoting of mutual love, that they might not wax cold when iniquity did abound. They spoke knowingly and edifyingly to one another for the increasing and improving of faith and holiness.

## II. THE MANNER IN WHICH GOD DIGNIFIED THE SAINTS.

## A. He Took Note of Their Conversation.

1. *The Lord was present with them.* He took notice of their pious discourses and was graciously present at their conferences. When the two disciples, going to Emmaus, were discoursing concerning Christ, He hearkened and heard and joined Himself to them and made a third (Luke 24:15).

2. *The Lord takes cognizance of all conversation.* God says that He hearkened and heard what bad men would say and that they spoke not right (Jeremiah 8:6); here He hearkened and heard what good men say and they spoke aright. God observes all the gracious words proceeding out of the mouths of His people, even in the most private conference, and He will reward openly.

## B. He Kept an Account of Them.

1. *The explanation.* "A book of remembrance was written before Him." Not that God needs to be reminded of things by books and writings, but it is an expression intimating that their pious affections and performances are kept in remembrance as punctually and particularly as if they were written in a book; as if journals were kept of all their conferences.

2. *The reason.* God remembers the services of His people in order that He may say, "Well done, enter thou into the joy of thy Lord" (Matthew 25:21). Never was any good word spoken of God or for God, from an honest heart, but it was registered in order that it might be recompensed in the resurrection of the just and in no wise lose its reward.

## C. He Promises to Them a Future Share in His Glory.

1. *The saints are God's jewels.* They are highly esteemed by Him and are dear to Him. They are comely with a comeliness that He puts upon them and He is pleased to glory in them. He looks upon them as His own proper goods, His choice goods, His treasure laid up in His cabinet. The rest of the world is but lumber in comparison with them

2. *The gathering up of God's jewels.* There is a day coming when God will make up His jewels. They shall be gathered up out of the dirt and gathered together from all places. All the saints will then be gathered to Christ, and none but saints, and saints made perfect. Then God's jewels will be made up as stones into a crown, as stars into a constellation.

3. *God's public confession of His saints.* Those who now own God for theirs, He will then own for His. He will publicly confess them before angels and men. "They shall be mine." Their relation to God shall be acknowledged. He will separate them from those that are not His and give them their portion with those who are His.

## D. He Promises to Them a Present Share in His Grace.

1. *The assurance of grace.* God had promised to own them as His and to take them to be with Him; but it might be a discouragement to them to think that they had offended God and He might justly disown them and cast them off; but, as to that, He says, "I will spare them," I will not deal with them as they deserve. The word usually signifies to spare with commiseration and compassion, as a father pitieth his children.

2. *The saints' duty in relation to God.* It is our duty to serve God with the disposition of children; we must be sons. We must be His servants. God will not have His children trained up in idleness. They must do Him service from the principle of love.

3. *The fatherly tenderness and compassion of God.* If we serve God with the disposition of children, He will spare us with the tenderness and compassion of a father. Even God's children that serve Him stand in need of sparing mercy, that mercy which has kept us from being consumed and which keeps us out of hell.

## CONCLUSION

When iniquity was bold and barefaced, the people of God took courage and stirred up themselves; when godliness was reproached and misrepresented, its friends did all they could to support it; when seducers were busy to deceive, they that feared the Lord were industrious to strengthen one another. Let us follow in the train of this godly remnant.

## 17

# *Forgiveness of Sin as a Debt*

> *And forgive us our debts.* —Matthew 6:12
> *And forgive us our sins.*    —Luke 11:4

FROM this petition in the Lord's prayer, thus differently expressed by the two evangelists, we may observe that sin is a debt to God and the pardon of sin is the forgiveness of this debt.

## I. SIN IS A DEBT TO GOD.

### A. The Manner in which Men Become Debtors to God.

1. *As the servant is indebted to his master.* Our Savior represents our case like that of a servant to a king who at the time of reckoning was found to be in debt to the king (Matthew 25:24-30).

2. *As the tenant is in debt to his landlord.* As a tenant who is behind in his rent or has damaged the landlord's property.

3. *As the borrower is indebted to the lender.* God has bestowed many mercies upon us, that is, He has been lending to us as the case has required.

4. *As the trespasser is indebted to the trespassed.* We have broken through the fences and bounds which God by His commands has set for us; therefore we are trespassers in debt to God.

5. *As the debt of a covenant breaker.* We have by solemn promise engaged ourselves to be the Lord's and to obey Him, but we have broken our covenant with God, so we are in debt to Him.

6. *As the debt of a malefactor to the law and to the government* when he is found guilty of treason or felony and consequently the law is to have its course against him.

7. *As the debt of an heir-at-law upon his ancestor's account,* that is, of a son who is liable to his father's debts after his death as far as his inheritance will go. By Adam's disobedience, we were all made sinners.

8. *As the debt of a surety upon account of the principle.* The guilt we have contracted by partaking of other men's sins, by being partners with them in sin.

B. **The Nature of the Debt of Sin.**

1. *It is an old debt.* The foundation of this debt was laid in Adam's sin and consequently we were born in debt.

2. *It is a just debt.* No matter how high the penalty is with which we are loaded it is less than our iniquities deserve.

3. *It is a great debt.* Until we return to God in repentance we continue to add to our debt, treasuring up unto ourselves guilt and wrath against the day of wrath.

C. **The Nature of the Debtors.**

1. *Careless and unconcerned.* Bad debtors are oftentimes careless and unconcerned about their debts. Thus sinners deal with their convictions, diverting them with the business of the world or drowning them in pleasures.

2. *Wasteful.* Sinners make waste of their time and opportunity and of the noble powers and faculties with which they are endued.

3. *Indifferent* toward creditors. Sinners take no pleasure in hearing from God, in speaking to Him, or in having anything to do with Him.

4. *Fearful.* Sinners carry about them a misgiving conscience which often reproaches them and fills them with secret terrors and bitterness.

5. *Dilatory and deceitful.* Bad debtors are apt to promise payment, but break their word. It is so with sinners.

D. The Danger of Debt.

1. *An account is kept of all of our debts.* If the debtor keeps not an account of his debts, yet the creditor does; they are all kept on record with God.

2. *Man is insolvent.* We are utterly insolvent and have not the wherewithal to pay our debts.

3. *No earthly friend to help.* Sinful men have no prospect of help from their fellowmen since they are in the same helpless condition and as deep in debt.

4. *Payment demanded.* The debts we owe to God are ever and anon demanded and the right is kept up by a continual claim.

5. *Death will arrest us for the debts.* Death is our discharge from other debts, but it lays us more open than ever to the debts against God. After death the judgment (Hebrews 9:27).

6. *The approach of the day of reckoning.* As sure as we see *this* day, we shall see *that* day when every man must give an account of himself unto God.

7. *Hell is the destination of debtors.* It is a pit of weeping and wailing and gnashing of teeth out of which there is no redemption.

II. THE FORGIVENESS OF DEBTS.

A. The Things Included in the Forgiveness of Sin as a Debt.

1. *God stays the process and does not allow the law to have its course.* Judgment is given against us, but execution is not taken out upon the judgment.

2. *God cancels the bond.* He pardons sin thoroughly and fully, so as to remember it no more against the sinner.

3. *God acquits the sinner.* This acquittal is delivered by the Spirit into the believer's hand, speaking peace to him, filling

him with comfort, arising from a sense of his justification and its tokens and pledges.

4. *God admits us to communion with Himself.* He condescends to deal with us again and to admit us into covenant and communion with Himself.

## B. The Ground of Hope for the Forgiveness of Sin as a Debt.

1. *The goodness of God.* We may ground our expectations upon the goodness of His nature (Psalm 86:5).

2. *The mediation of Christ.* God forgives our debt because Jesus Christ by the blood of His cross has made satisfaction for it.

## C. The Requirement for the Forgiveness of Sin as a Debt.

1. *Confess the debt.* This confession of debt must be specific and accompanied with godly sorrow.

2. *Acknowledge the judgment of all we have to Christ.* Our own selves we must give unto the Lord, and for us to live must be Christ.

3. *Honor Christ.* We must disclaim all dependence upon our sufficiency and rest upon Christ only as a complete and all-sufficient Savior.

4. *Study what we shall render to Christ.* Take all occasions to speak of that great love wherewith He loved us.

5. *Engage ourselves for the future,* that we will render to God the things that are His and be careful not to run into debt again.

6. *Forgiveness of others.* God will have His children to be like Him, merciful and good.

## CONCLUSION

Oh that the love of Christ may constrain us to love Him and live for Him who loved us and died for us.

# 18

## *Laying up Treasure*

> *Lay not up for yourselves treasures upon earth: but lay up for yourselves treasures in heaven: for where your treasure is, there will your heart be also.*
> —Matthew 6:19-21

WORLDLY-MINDEDNESS is as common and as fatal a symptom of hypocrisy as any other, for by no sin can Satan have a surer and faster hold of the soul, under the cloak of a visible and passable profession of Christianity than by this. Therefore, Christ proceeds to warn us against coveting the wealth of the world.

## I. GOOD CAUTION.

**A. The Meaning of Treasure.** A treasure is an abundance of something that is in itself, at least in our opinion, precious and valuable and likely to stand us in good stead hereafter. It is that something which the soul will have, which it looks upon as the best thing, which it has a complacency and confidence in above all other things.

**B. The Prohibition against Laying up Earthly Treasures.** "Lay not up for yourselves treasures upon earth." A good caution against making the things that are seen and that are temporal our best things and placing our happiness in them. Christ's disciples had left all to follow Him, let them still keep in the same good mind.

**C. The Explanation of the Prohibition Against Laying up Earthly Treasure.**

1. *Earthly treasures should not be considered the best things.* We must not count these things the best things, not the most valuable in themselves, nor the most serviceable to us. We must not call them glory, as Laban's sons did (Genesis 31:1), but see and own that they have no glory in comparison with the glory that excelleth (II Corinthians 3:10).

2. *Abundance of earthly treasures should not be coveted.* We must not covet an abundance of these things nor be still grasping at more and more of them, and adding to them, as men do that which is their treasure, as never knowing when we have enough.

3. *Earthly treasures should not be trusted in for security.* We must not confide in earthly treasures for futurity, to be our security and supply in time to come. We must not say to the gold, "Thou art my hope."

4. *Earthly treasures should not content us.* We must not content ourselves with them as all we need or desire. We must be content with a little for our passage through life, but not with all for our portion. These things must not be made our consolation, our good things. Let us consider that we are laying up, not for posterity in this world, but for ourselves in the other world.

## II. GOOD COUNSEL.

A. The Substance of the Counsel. "Lay up for yourselves treasures in heaven." This good counsel is an entreaty to make the joys and glories of the other world, those things not seen that are eternal, our best things and to place our happiness in them.

B. The Implications of the Counsel.

1. *The certainty of the heavenly treasures.* There are treasures in heaven as sure as there are on this earth; and those in heaven are the only true treasures, the riches and glories and pleasures that are at God's right hand, which those who are sanctified truly arrive at when they come to be perfectly sanctified in heaven.

2. *The wisdom of laying up heavenly treasures.* It is our wisdom to lay up our treasure in those heavenly treasures; to give all diligence to make sure our title to eternal life through Jesus Christ and to depend upon that as our happiness and look upon all things here below with a holy contempt, as not worthy to be compared with it. Let us not burden ourselves with the cash of this world, but lay up in store good securities.

3. *The security of the heavenly treasures.* It is a great encouragement to us to lay up treasure in heaven in knowing that there it is safe. It will not decay of itself, no moth or rust will corrupt it; nor can we be by force or fraud deprived of it; thieves do not break through and steal. It is a happiness above and beyond the changes and chances of time. It is an inheritance that is incorruptible (I Peter 1:4).

## III. GOOD REASONS.

### A. Against Laying up Earthly Treasures.

1. *Because they are liable to loss and decay by internal corruption.* That which is treasure upon earth moth and rust corrupts. If the treasure be laid up in fine clothes, the moth eats them and they are spoiled. Gold and silver tarnishes and grows less with using. Worldly riches have in themselves a principle of corruption and decay; they wither of themselves and make themselves wings.

2. *Because they are liable to loss and decay by external violence.* "Thieves break through and steal." Every hand of violence will be aiming at the house where the treasure of this world is laid up; nor can anything be laid up so safe, but we may be spoiled of it. It is folly to make that our treasure of which we may so easily be robbed.

### B. In Favor of Laying up Heavenly Treasures.

1. *Because it affects our thoughts.* "Where your treasure is," on earth or in heaven, "there will your heart be." We are therefore concerned to be right and wise in the choice of our treasure, because the temper of our minds will be

accordingly, either carnal or spiritual, earthly or heavenly. Where the treasure is, there is the love and affection (Colossians 3:2).

2. *Because it affects our lives.* The way the desires and pursuits go, thitherward the aims and intents are levelled, and all is done with that in view. Where a treasure is, there our cares and fears are, lest we come short of it; about that we are more solicitous; there our hope and trust is; there our joys and delights will be.

## CONCLUSION

If we know and consider ourselves what we are, what we are made for, how long our continuance, and that our souls are ourselves, we shall see it a foolish thing to lay up treasure on earth. Acceptance with God is treasure in heaven which can neither be corrupted nor stolen. If we have thus laid up treasure with Him, with Him our hearts will be.

**19**

# *A Three-fold Invitation*

> *Come unto me all ye that labor and are heavy laden, and I will give you rest. Take my yoke upon you, and learn of me; for I am meek and lowly in heart: and ye shall find rest unto your soul: for my yoke is easy, and my burden is light.*
>
> —Matthew 11:28-30

HERE is an offer that is made to us and an invitation to accept it. After so solemn a preface (verses 25-27) we may well expect something very great; and it is so, a faithful saying and well worthy of all acceptation; words whereby we may be saved. We are here invited to Christ as our priest, prince, and prophet; to be saved, to be ruled, to be taught by Him.

## I. AN INVITATION TO REST. Verse 28.

### A. The Character of the Persons Invited.

1. *The description.* "All that labor and are heavy laden." All those and only those are invited to rest in Christ who are sensible to sin as a burden and groan under it, who are not only convinced of the evil of sin, but are contrite in soul for it; that are really sick of their sins, weary of the service of the world and of the flesh.

2. *The illustrations.* Ephraim who bemoaned his sins (Jeremiah 31:18-20); the prodigal and the publican who confessed their condition (Luke 15:17; 18:13); Peter's hearers who were pricked in their hearts (Acts 2:37); and the Philippian jailor who trembled (Acts 16:29-30). This is a necessary preparation for pardon and peace. The Com-

82

forter must first convince (John 16:8) and then He will deal.

## B. The Substance of the Invitation.

1. *The call given.* "Come unto me." We must accept Him as our Physician and Advocate; freely willing to be saved by Him, in His own way, and upon His own terms. Come and cast thy burden upon Him. This is the Gospel call, "The Spirit and the bride say, Come. And let him that heareth say, Come. And let him that is athirst come. And whosoever will, let him take the water of life freely" (Revelation 22:17).

2. *The blessing promised.* "I will give you rest." Jesus Christ will give assured rest to those weary souls who by a living faith come to Him for it; rest from the terror of sin, in a well-grounded peace of conscience; rest from the power of sin, in a regular order of the soul and its due government of itself; a rest in God and a complacency of soul in His love.

## II. AN INVITATION TO SUBMISSION. Verse 29.

## A. The Significance of the Yoke.

1. *It is Christ's yoke.* We must come to Jesus Christ as our ruler and submit ourselves to Him. To call those who are weary and heavy laden to take a yoke upon them looks like adding affliction to the afflicted; but the pertinency of it lies in the word *My*. "You are under a yoke which makes you weary, shake that off and try mine, which will make you easy."

2. *It suggests service and submission.* Servants and subjects are said to be under the yoke (I Timothy 6:1; I Kings 12:10). To take Christ's yoke upon us is to put ourselves into the relation of servants and subjects to Him and then to conduct ourselves accordingly, in a conscientious obedience to all His commands and a cheerful submission to all His disposals. It is to obey the gospel of Christ.

**B. The Nature of the Yoke and Burden.**

1. *It is an easy yoke.* The yoke of Christ's commands is an easy yoke; it is not only easy, but gracious. It is sweet and pleasant. There is nothing in it to gall the yielding neck, nothing to hurt us, but on the contrary, much to refresh us. It is a yoke that is lined with love. His commands are so reasonable and profitable.

2. *It is a light burden.* The afflictions from Christ which befall us as men and, especially, afflictions for Christ which befall us as Christians constitute the burden of Christ. This burden in itself is not joyous, but grievous; yet as it is Christ's, it is light. Paul knew as much of it as any man and he calls it a light affliction. God's presence, Christ's sympathy, and especially the Spirit's aids and comforts make suffering for Christ light and easy.

**III. AN INVITATION TO LEARN. Verses 29-30.**

**A. The Conditions to be Met in Order to Learn.**

1. *We must will to learn.* We must come to Jesus Christ as our Teacher and set ourselves to learn of Him. Christ has erected a great school and has invited us to be His scholars. We must enter ourselves and associate with His scholars.

2. *We must heed His teaching.* We must daily heed the instructions He gives by His Word and Spirit. We must converse much with what He said and have it ready to use upon all occasions. We must conform to what He did and follow His steps (I Peter 2:21).

**B. The Reasons Given for Learning.**

1. *Christ is worthy to teach.* "I am meek and lowly in heart" and therefore fit to teach you. He is meek and can have compassion on the ignorant. Many able teachers are hot and hasty, which is a discouragement to those who are dull and slow; but Christ knows how to bear with such and to open their understandings. He is lowly in heart. He condescends to teach poor scholars and novices. He teaches the first principles and stoops to the most humble capacities.

2. *The effect of Christ's teaching.* Rest for the soul is the most desirable rest. The only sure way of finding this rest is to sit at Christ's feet and hear His word. The way of duty is the way of rest. The understanding finds rest in the knowledge of God and Jesus Christ. The effections find rest in the love of God and Jesus Christ. This rest is to be had with Christ for all those who learn of Him.

## CONCLUSION

This is the sum and substance of the gospel, the call and offer. We are told, in a few words, what the Lord Jesus requires of us and it agrees with what God said of Him once and again: "This is my beloved Son, in whom I am well pleased; hear ye Him."

# 20

# *The Angel's Resurrection Message*

> *And the angel answered and said unto the women, Fear not ye: for I know that ye seek Jesus, which was crucified. He is not here: for He is risen, as He said. Come, see the place where the Lord lay: and go quickly, and tell His disciples that He is risen from the dead.* —Matthew 28:5-7

WE MAY THINK that it would have been better if a competent number of witnesses would have been present to see the resurrection of the Lord Jesus; but let us not prescribe to God, who ordered that the witnesses of His resurrection should see Him risen, but not see Him rise.

## I. THE ENCOURAGEMENT AGAINST FEARS. Verse 5.

**A. The Circumstances.** To come near to graves and tombs, especially in silence and solitude, has something in it that is frightful. Much more was it to these women, to find an angel at the sepulchre.

1. *The solitude of the sepulchre.*

2. *The presence of an angel.*

**B. The Reassurance.**

1. *The expression of the reassurance.* The keepers shook and became as dead men (verse 4), but, fear not ye. Let the sinners in Zion be afraid (Isaiah 33:14), for there is cause for it; but fear not ye faithful seed of Abraham. Why should the daughters of Sarah, that do well, be afraid with any amazement (I Peter 3:6)?

2. *The reason for the reassurance.* "Fear not ye. Let not the news I have to tell you, be any surprise to you; for ye were told before that your Master would rise. Let it be no terror to you, for His resurrection will be your consolation. Fear not ye, for I know that ye seek Jesus. I know you are friends to the cause."

## II. THE ASSURANCE OF THE RESURRECTION OF CHRIST. Verse 6.

### A. The Fact of the Resurrection.

1. *The statement.* "He is not here, for He is risen." He is not dead, but alive again; we cannot as yet show you Him, hereafter you will see Him. To be told, "He is not here," would have been no welcome news to those who sought Him, if it had not been added, "He is risen."

2. *The warning.* We must not hearken to those who say "Lo, here is Christ or Lo, He is there," for He is not *here*, He is not *there*, He is *risen*. In all of our inquiries after Christ, we must remember that He is risen and we must seek Him as one who is risen.

### B. The Proof of His Resurrection.

1. *The evidence of the empty tomb.* "Come and see where the Lord lay. You see that He is not here and remembering what He said you may be satisfied that He is risen. Come see the place and you will see that He is not there, you will see that He could not be stolen thence and therefore must conclude that He is risen."

2. *The comfort of the empty tomb.* It may have a good influence upon us if we come and with an eye of faith see the place where the Lord lay. See the marks He has left there of His love in condescending so low for us. When we look into the grave where we expect to lie, to take off the terror of it, let us look into the grave where the Lord lay.

### C. The Importance of His Resurrection.

1. *It is the fulfilment of the Word of Christ.* The angel, when he said, "He is not here, He is risen," reveals to us that

he preaches no other gospel than what He had already received, for he refers himself to the Word of Christ as sufficient to bear him out. "He is risen as He said."

2. *It is the proper object of faith.* This he vouches as the proper object of faith: "He said that He would rise and you know that He is the Truth itself and therefore have reason to expect that He should rise. Why should you be backward to believe that which He told you would be?"

## III. THE RESPONSIBILITY IN VIEW OF THE RESURRECTION OF CHRIST. Verse 7

### A. The News of the Resurrection Must Be Proclaimed.

1. *To encourage the disciples.* "Tell His disciples" in order that they may be comforted; that they may encourage themselves under their present sorrows. It was a dismal time with them, between grief and fear; what a cordial would this be to them now, to hear that their Master is risen!

2. *To revivify the disciples.* This news was told to them in order that they may enquire further into themselves. This message was sent to them to awaken them from that strange stupidity which had seized them and to raise their expectations. This was to set them on seeking Him and to prepare them for His appearance to them.

### B. The News of the Resurrection Must Be Proclaimed by its Witnesses.

1. *The vessels chosen for the proclamation of the resurrection.* The women were sent to tell the news of the resurrection to the disciples. Still God chooses the weak things of the world to confound the mighty (I Corinthians 1:27) and puts the treasure not only in earthen vessels (II Corinthians 4:7), but here into the weaker vessels (I Peter 3:7).

2. *The honor of the proclamation of the resurrection.* This was an honor placed upon them and a recompense for their constant affectionate adherence to Him at the cross and in the grave, and a rebuke to the disciples who forsook Him.

## C. The Required Obedience to the Command Must Be Immediate.

1. *The reason for the immediacy.* They were bid to go quickly upon this errand. Why, what haste was there? Would not the news be welcome at any time? Yes, but the disciples were now overwhelmed with grief and Christ would have this cordial hastened to them. When Daniel was humbling himself before God for sin, the angel Gabriel was caused to fly swiftly with a message of comfort (Daniel 9:27).

2 *The required readiness.* We must always be ready: (a) to obey the commands of God; (b) to do good to our brethren and to carry comfort to them, as those that felt from their afflictions: "Say not, Go and come again, and tomorrow I will give," but now quickly.

## CONCLUSION

In the preceding two chapters of Matthew (26 and 27) we see the Captain of our salvation engaged with the powers of darkness and our Champion fell before them. The powers of darkness seem to ride as masters, but then the Lord arose. The Prince of Peace comes out of the grave a Conqueror, yea, more than a conqueror. He lives!

**21**

## A Sermon on Disputes

> *What was it that ye disputed among your-*
> *selves by the way?* —Mark 9:33

OUR Lord Jesus is here calling His disciples to an account about a warm debate they happened to have among themselves, as they traveled along, upon a question often started, but
not yet determined, *Which of them should be the greatest?*

### I. ALL BELIEVERS MUST EXPECT TO BE CALLED TO AN ACCOUNT BY OUR LORD.

**A. The Present Life Determines the Future.** Believers are
travelers, under the conduct of our great Master, towards the
better country; and according as our steps are, while we are
in the way, our rest will be when we are at our journey's end.

**B. The Present Works and Words Will be Reviewed in the
Future.** Every work and every word will be brought into
judgment, will be weighed in a just and unerring balance, will
be produced in evidence for us or against us.

**C. The Judge Will be the Lord Jesus Christ.**

1. *The fact stated.* The account must be given to our Lord
Jesus. To Him the Father has committed all judgment
(John 5:22; II Corinthians 5:9-10).

2. *The lessons implied.* Therefore we should judge ourselves
and prove our own work. It is also a good reason why
we should not judge one another or be severe in our
censures of one another.

## II. ALL BELIEVERS MUST GIVE AN ACCOUNT OF THEIR CONVERSATIONS AMONG THEMSELVES.

**A. Christ Takes Note of our Conversation.** For "every idle word that men shall speak they shall give account thereof in the day of judgment. For by thy words thou shalt be justified and by thy words thou shalt be condemned" (Matthew 12:36, 37).

**B. Christ Takes Note of our Edifying Conversation.** There is not a good word coming from a good heart and directed to a good end, but is heard in secret and shall be rewarded openly (Malachi 3:16).

**C. Christ Takes Note of our Corrupt Conversation.** If any corrupt communication proceeds out of our mouths Christ observes it and is displeased and we shall hear of it again.

## III. ALL BELIEVERS WILL ESPECIALLY BE CALLED TO GIVE AN ACCOUNT OF THEIR DISPUTES.

**A. An Explanation of Disputes.**

1. *The meaning.* Disputing supposes some variance and strife, and a mutual contradiction and opposition arising from it.

2. *The classification.* (a) There are disputes that are of use among Christians; for example, for the conviction of unbelievers, the confirmation of those in danger of being led astray. (b) There are also disputes which cannot be vindicated and of which we are ashamed.

**B. The Occasions of Disputes.**

1. *Differences of opinion.* Disputes commonly arise from differences of opinion, either in religion and divine things; or in philosophy, politics, or other parts of learning; or in the conduct of human life.

2. *Separate and interfering interests in this world.* Neighbors and relatives quarrel about their rights and properties, their estates and trades, their honors and powers and pleasures. These disputes, as they are the most common, so they are the most scandalous.

3. *Passion and clashing tempers.* Some indulge themselves in a crossness of temper that makes them continually uneasy to all about them. They love to thwart and disagree and to dispute everything, though ever so plain or trifling.

## C. Proper Conduct in Disputes.

1. *Be on the side of truth and right.* As far as we are able to make a judgment, let us see to it that we have the truth and right on our side and not be confident and further than we see just cause to be so.

2. *If doubtful remember you may be wrong.* In matters of doubtful disputation, while contending for that which we take to be right, let us think it possible that we may be in the wrong.

3. *Have full control of yourself.* Let us carefully suppress all inward tumults, whatever provocation may be given us; and let our minds be calm and sedate in whatever argument we are engaged.

4. *Observe proper charity.* Let us in all of our disputes keep ourselves under the commanding power and influence of holy love; for that victory is dearly purchased, that is obtained at the expense of Christian charity.

5. *Remember the account that must be given to our Lord.* Often think of the account we must shortly give to our great Master of all of our disputes with our fellow-servants by the way.

## IV. ALL BELIEVERS WILL BE MOST STRICTLY RECKONED WITH FOR THEIR DISPUTES ABOUT SUPREMACY.

### A. The Disciples' Subject of Dispute.
It was about precedency and superiority — "Who should be the greatest?"

### B. The Lord's Attitude toward the Disciples' Dispute.
He is displeased with them because it is an indication that they aimed at being great in the world.

### C. The Reasons for Our Lord's Displeasure Concerning the Disciples' Dispute.

1. *It was the result of a mistaken notion of Christ's kingdom.* The disciples had imbibed the notion that our Lord Jesus, though He appeared meanly at first, would soon reign over a temporal kingdom.

2. *It was contrary to His laws of humility and love.* It is against the law of humility to covet to be great in this world and against the law of love to strive who shall be greatest.

3. *It was contrary to the example set by the Lord Jesus.* The same mind should have been in them that was in Him who "made Himself of no reputation (emptied Himself)" and who washed the disciples' feet (Philippians 2:7; John 13:45).

4. *It would render them unfit for their appointed service.* It was very absurd for the disciples to strive who should be greatest when they were all to labor and suffer reproach and poverty and ignominy.

5. *It was a corrupt temper that would be the bane of the church.* It would be the reproach of its ministry, an obstruction to its enlargement, the disturbance of its peace and the original of all the breaches that would be made upon its order and unity.

## CONCLUSION

Let us never strive who shall be greatest in this world for it is despicable and dangerous; but let all our strife be who shall be best. Especially let us strive to excel ourselves and to do more good than we have done (Philippians 3:13, 14).

**22**

## Christ's Discourse on Regeneration

> *Except a man be born again, he cannot see the kingdom of God. Except a man be born of water and of the Spirit, he cannot enter into the kingdom of God. The wind bloweth where it listeth, and thou hearest the sound thereof, but cannot tell whence it cometh, and wither it goeth: so is everyone that is born of the Spirit.*   —John 3:3,5,8

Nᴏᴛ MANY mighty and noble are called, yet some are, and here was one. This was a man of the Pharisees, bred to learning, a scholar. The principles of the Pharisees and peculiarities of their sect were directly contrary to the spirit of Christianity; yet there were some in whom even those high thoughts were cast down and brought into obedience to Christ. It was in response to Nicodemus' visit that the Lord Jesus discourses on the new birth.

### I. THE NATURE OF REGENERATION.

**A. It is a New Life.** Birth is the beginning of life; to be born again is to begin anew, as those that have hitherto lived either much amiss or to little purpose. We must not think to patch up the old building, but begin from the foundation.

**B. It is a New Nature.**

1. *We must be born anew.* We must have a new nature, new principles, new affections, new aims. We must be born anew. By our first birth we were corrupt, shapen in sin and iniquity; we must therefore undergo a second birth, our souls must be fashioned and enlivened anew.

2. *We must be born from above.* This new birth has its rise from heaven: "Which were born, not of blood, nor of the will of the flesh, nor of the will of man, but of God" (John 1:13). Its tendency is to heaven; it is to be born to a divine and heavenly life, a life of communion with God and the upper world, and in order to do this, it is to partake of a divine nature and bear the image of the heavenly.

## II. THE NECESSITY FOR REGENERATION.

**A. This is Seen in that Christ Declared It.** Christ has said it and as He himself never did nor ever will abrogate it, so all the world cannot gainsay it. He who is the great Lawgiver and the great Mediator of the new covenant and the great Physician of souls, who knows man's case and what is necessary to his cure, has said: "Ye must be born again."

**B. This is Seen in that We Cannot Understand the Nature of the Kingdom of God without Regeneration.** Such is the nature of the things pertaining to the kingdom of God (in which Nicodemus desired to be instructed) that the soul must be new modelled and moulded; the natural man must become a spiritual man before he is capable of receiving and understanding them. "But the natural man receiveth not the things of the Spirit of God: for they are foolishness unto him: neither can he know them, because they are spiritually discerned" (I Corinthians 2:14).

**C. This is Seen in that We Cannot Receive the Comfort of the Kingdom of God without Regeneration.** We cannot without the new birth, receive the comfort of it; cannot expect any benefit by Christ and His gospel which is absolutely necessary to our happiness here and hereafter. Considering what we are by nature, how corrupt and sinful; what God is, in whom alone we can be happy; and what heaven is, to which the perfection of our happiness is reserved; it will appear in the nature of the thing that we must be born again; because it is impossible that we should be happy, if we are not holy.

1. *Because of what we are.*

2. *Because of what God is.*

3. *Because of what heaven is.*

## III. THE METHOD OF REGENERATION.

### A. The Method Stated.

1. *What it is not.* It is not wrought by any wisdom or power of our own. "Not of works, lest any man should boast" (Ephesians 2:9). "Not by works of righteousness which we have done" (Titus 3:5).

2. *What it is.* To be born again is to be born of the Spirit. It is wrought by the power and influence of the blessed Spirit of Grace. It is the sanctification of the Spirit (I Peter 1:2) and renewing of the Holy Spirit (Titus 3:5). The word He works by is His inspiration and the heart to be wrought on He has access to. Those who are regenerated by the Spirit are made spiritual and refined from the dross and dregs of sensuality.

### B. The Method Illustrated.

1. *It is compared to water.* To be born again is to be born of water and of the Spirit, that is, of the Spirit working like water. That which is intended here is to show that the Spirit, in sanctifying a soul (1) cleanses and purifies it as water; takes away its filth by which it was unfit for the kingdom of God. It is the washing of regeneration (Titus 3:5); (2) cools and refreshes the soul as water does the hunted hart and the weary traveller.

2. *It is compared to wind.* The Holy Spirit's work in regeneration compared to wind indicates: (1) The Spirit works arbitrarily and as a free agent. The wind blows where it will and is not subject to our command, but is directed of God. The Spirit dispenses His influences on whom and in what measure and degree He pleases. (2) He works powerfully and with evident effects. (3) He works mysteriously and in secret, hidden ways. The manner and methods of the Spirit's working are a mystery.

## CONCLUSION

"Ye must be born again."   Christ shows that it is necessary in the nature of the thing, for we are not fit to enter into the kingdom of God until we are born again.   "That which is born of the flesh is flesh."   Here is our malady and the causes of it, which are such as speak plainly that there is no remedy but the new birth.

# 23

## *Faith in Christ Inferred from Faith in God*

> *Ye believe in God, believe also in me.*
> —John 14:1

THAT which is here intended as a comfort in time of trouble will not be so unless it be our practice, for it is our duty at all times not only to believe in God, but to believe also in Jesus Christ.

## I. THE OBJECTS OF FAITH.

A. **God the Father Almighty and Christ the Father's Only Begotten Son.** We cannot believe in God as the Father without believing in Him who is the Son of the Father, the only begotten of the Father and therefore of the same nature with Him.

B. **God the Eternal Mind and Christ the Eternal Word and Wisdom.** God is an infinite Spirit and He has told us that the Redeemer is the Word. As the thought is one with the mind that thinks it and yet may be considered as distinct from it, so Christ was and is one with the Father and yet distinct from the Eternal Wisdom.

C. **God the Creator and Governor of the World and Christ the Power of God.** Nothing appears more evident by the light of the Gospel than the fact that God made the worlds by His Son and by Him all things consist (hold together).

D. **God our Owner by the Right of Creation, Christ our Owner by the Right of Redemption.** As to God we owe our being because He made us; so to Christ we owe our well

98

being, our recovery from that deplorable state into which we
were plunged by sin.

E. **God our Judge and Christ our Advocate.** We are conscious
that we are sinners and that from God our judgment must
proceed.  Whenever we think of giving an account to God we
must remember the Lord Jesus as the only mediator between
us and God.

F. **God our End and Christ our Way.** We know that God
who made us is He for whom we are made and He is alone
able to make us happy.  The Gospel tells us that Christ is the
true and living way to the Father (John 14:6).

## II. THE ACTS OF FAITH.

A. **Acquaintance with God and with Christ.** We think we are
concerned to know God; we are, but that will not be life eternal
to us, unless withal we know Jesus Christ whom the Father
has sent to acquaint us with Him.

B. **Adoration of God and Christ.** Those who believe in God
as Sovereign Lord will see themselves obliged to give Him
the glory due to His name and to pay their homage to Him.
And thus we must express our faith in Christ as the restored
blind man: "Lord, I believe; and he worshipped Him" (John
9:38).

C. **Reverence of God and Christ.** If we believe in the majesty
of God we shall tremble at His presence and be afraid of fall-
ing under His displeasure, much more of remaining under it.
Let us also believe in Christ and thus express it.

D. **Study to do the Will of God and Christ.** All who believe
in God study to do His will and we must also study to do the
will of Christ and in the temper of our minds and tenor of our
lives to comply with it.

E. **Delight Ourselves in God and Christ.** Since, through faith,
we rejoice in God, so believing we must rejoice also in Christ;
for in Him dwell not only the awful, but all the amiable perfections of the divine nature.  It is in Christ Jesus that we
rejoice and in God through Him.

F. **Dependence and Confidence in God and Christ.** We rely
upon God to direct us, to support and strengthen us, to pity us;
and now let us thus believe also in Jesus Christ and make Him
our hope.

## III. THE NECESSARY CONNECTION BETWEEN FAITH IN GOD AND IN CHRIST.

A. **If We Believe in God We Must Believe in Christ Who is
One with the Father.** Christ has told us, "I and My Father are one" (John 10:30). We come to the knowledge of
God by the knowledge of Jesus Christ and whoever believes
in the Father, as far as the Son is revealed to him to be one
with the Father, will believe also in Him.

B. **If We Believe in God We Must Believe in Christ Who has
been Commissioned, Sent and Testified to by God.** We do
not believe in God unless we believe what He has said concerning His Son and rest upon it (Luke 10:16; Matthew 3:17;
John 5:30).

C. **If We Believe in God We Must Honor Him by Believing
in Christ.** If we confess that Jesus Christ is Lord, it is to
the glory of God the Father (Philippians 2:11).

D. **If We Believe that God Spoke by Moses and the Prophets
We Must Believe in Christ of Whom They Bear Testimony.** All the prophets bear witness to Christ and in all
the ceremonies of Mosaic institution He was typified. Our
Lord insisted that one of the strongest proofs of His divine
mission was the Old Testament Scriptures.

E. **If We Rightly Apprehend how Matters Stand between
God and Man since the Fall We Will Believe the Gospel
Record of a Mediator between God and Man.**

1. *Man in a great measure has lost the knowledge of God.* We
cannot but perceive that man has in a great measure lost
the knowledge of God and therefore he should gladly believe
in Christ who has revealed God to us.

2. *There is an infinite distance between God and man.* The
light of nature shows us the glory of a God above us;
whence we all are tempted to infer that we cannot have

communion with Him. Shall we not therefore welcome the tidings of a Mediator between God and man?

3. *There is a quarrel between God and man because of sin.* The God who made us is not only above us, but against us; and therefore we should gladly believe in Him by whom that quarrel is taken up, in whom God was reconciling the world to Himself (II Corinthians 5:19).

4. *Man is corrupt and sinful.* We find by daily experience that our minds are alienated from God and there is in them a strong bias toward the world and the flesh; that we are not of ourselves inclinable to or sufficient for anything that is good.

5. *Man's spirit is immortal.* If we believe that God is the Father of our spirits we cannot but perceive that they are immortal and we are made for another world and therefore we will gladly believe in One who will be our Guide to that world.

## CONCLUSION

Let that be the language of our settled judgments which a learned and religious man took for his motto: "Christ is a Christian's all." Let a martyr's testimony be the language of our pious affections: "None but Christ, none but Christ."

# 24

# *Wonderful Love*

> *As the Father hath loved me, so have I*
> *loved you: continue ye in my love.*
> —John 15:9

IT IS generally agreed that Christ's discourse in this and the next chapter was at the close of His Last Supper, the night in which He was betrayed. Now that He was about to leave the disciples, they would be tempted to grow strange to one another and therefore He presses it upon them to love one another.

## I. THE FATHER'S LOVE FOR CHRIST.

**A. The Fact of the Father's Love for His Son.** "As the Father hath loved me." He loved Him as Mediator: "This is my beloved Son" (Matthew 3:17; 17:5). He was the Son of His love. He loved Him and gave all things into His hands (John 13:3).

**B. The Son's Abiding in His Father's Love.**

1. *He continuously loved the Father.* He continually loved His Father and was beloved of Him. Even when He was made sin and a curse for us and it pleased the Lord to bruise Him, yet He abode in the Father's love.

2. *He cheerfully suffered because He loved the Father.* Because He continued to love His Father, He went cheerfully through His sufferings, and therefore His Father continued to love Him.

**C. The Requisite for Christ to Abide in His Father's Love.**

1. *Obedience was required.* He abode in His Father's love because He kept His Father's law: "I have kept my Father's commandments, and abide in His love" (verse 10).

102

2. *Obedience manifested His love.*  Hereby He showed that
He continued to love His Father, that He went on and
went through with His undertaking.  Therefore the Father
continued to love Him.  His soul delighted in Him because
He did not fail, nor was discouraged (Isaiah 42:1, 4).

## II. THE SON'S LOVE FOR HIS DISCIPLES.

### A. The Pattern of His Love.

1. *The love as a Son.*  "As the Father hath loved me, so
have I loved you."  A strange expression of the condescending grace of Christ!  As the Father loved Him who was
most worthy, He loved them who were most unworthy.
The Father loved Him as His Son and He loves them as
His children.

2. *The love that gave all things.*  "The Father gave all things
into His hands," so with Himself, He freely gives us all
things.  The Father loved Him as Mediator, as head of the
Church, and the great trustee of divine grace and favor,
which He had not for Himself only, but for the benefit of
those for whom He was intrusted; and He says, "I have
been a faithful trustee.  As the Father has committed His
love to Me, so I transmit it to you."

### B. The Proofs and Products of His Love.

1. *Christ's voluntary death.*  Christ loved His disciples, for
He laid down His life for them.  Others have laid down
their lives, content that their lives should be taken from
them; but Christ gave up His life, was not merely passive,
but made it His own act and deed.

2. *Christ's covenant of friendship.*  The followers of Christ
are the friends of Christ.  He is graciously pleased to call
and count them so.  They that do the duty of His servants
are admitted and advanced to the dignity of His friends
(verses 14-15).  He is afflicted in their afflictions and takes
pleasure in their prosperity.

3. *His communication of His mind to the disciples.* "All things that I have heard of My Father I have made known unto you" (verse 15). As to the secret will of God, there are many things which we must be content not to know; but as to the revealed will of God, Jesus Christ has faithfully handed to us what He received of the Father.

4. *His choosing men to represent Him on the earth.* Christ loved His disciples, for He chose and ordained them to be the prime instruments of His glory and honor in the world (verse 16). It is fitting that Christ should have the choosing of His own ministers; still He does it by His providence and Spirit.

## III. THE DISCIPLES' LOVE FOR CHRIST.

### A. It is to be a Continuous Love. "Continue in your love to me and in mine to you."

1. *They are to continue to love Him.* All that love Christ should continue in their love to Him, that is, be always loving Him and taking all occasions to show it, and to love to the end.

2. *They are to continue in His love.* We must place our happiness in the continuance of Christ's love to us and make it our business to give continued proofs of our love to Christ, that nothing may tempt us to withdraw from Him or provoke Him to withdraw from us.

### B. It is to be a Joyous Love.

1. *Abiding joy.* The words "that my joy might remain in you" (verse 11) are so placed in the original that they may mean: (a) "My joy in you may remain." If they bring forth fruit and continue in His love He will continue to rejoice in them. (b) "Your joy in me may remain." It is the will of Christ that His disciples should constantly rejoice in Him (Philippians 4:4).

2. *Fulness of joy.* Not only that you might be full of joy, but that your joy in Christ and in His love may rise higher and

higher until it comes to perfection, when "ye enter into the joy of your Lord."

## C. It is to an Obedient Love.

1. *The promise.* "Ye shall abide in my love" (verse 10), as in a dwelling place, at home in Christ's love; as in a resting place, at ease in Christ's love; as in a strong-hold, safe in God's love. "Ye shall abide in my love," you shall have grace and strength to persevere in loving Christ.

2. *The condition of the promise.* "If ye keep my commandments" (verse 10). The disciples were to keep Christ's commandments, not only by constant conformity to themselves; but by a faithful delivery of them to others; they were to keep them as trustees in whose hands the great deposit was lodged. They were to teach all things that Christ had commanded (Matthew 28:20).

## CONCLUSION

The surest evidence of our love to Christ is obedience to the laws of Christ. Such are loved by the Father and the Son. Both of these loves are the crown and comfort, the grace and glory which shall be to all them that love the Lord Jesus Christ in sincerity.

## 25

# The Benefits of Justification

*Therefore being justified by faith, we have
peace with God . . . we have access by faith
. . . rejoice in the glory of God . . . we glory
in tribulations.* —Romans 5:1-5

THE PRECIOUS benefits and privileges which flow
from justification are such as should quicken us all to give diligence to make it sure to ourselves that we are justified and then
to take the comfort it renders to us and to do the duty it calls
from us. The fruits of this tree of life are exceeding precious.

## I. WE HAVE PEACE WITH GOD. Verse 1.

**A. The Condition of Man Reveals his Need for Peace.** It is
sin that breeds the quarrel between us and God, creates not
only a strangeness, but an enmity. The holy, righteous God
cannot in honor be at peace with a sinner while he continues
under the guilt of sin. Justification takes away the guilt and
so makes way for peace. And such are the benignity and
good will of God to man that immediately upon the removal
of the obstacle the peace is made.

**B. The Character of the Peace of the Justified Man.** There is
more in this peace than barely a cessation of enmity, there
is friendship and loving kindness, for God is either the worst
enemy or the best friend. Abraham being justified by faith
was called the friend of God (James 2:23), which was his
honor, but not his peculiar honor; Christ has called His disciples friends (John 15:13-15). Surely a man needs no more
to make him happy than to have God as his friend.

106

**C. The Channel by which Peace is Brought to Man.** This peace is through our Lord Jesus Christ; through Him as our great Peacemaker, the Mediator between God and man (I Timothy 2:5), that blessed Daysman that has laid His hand upon us both. "He is our peace" (Ephesians 2:14), not only the Maker, but the matter and maintenance of our peace (Colossians 1:20).

## II. WE HAVE ACCESS TO GOD. Verse 2.

**A. The Saints' Happy State.** It is a state of grace, God's loving kindness to us and our conformity to God. Now "unto this grace we have access" — an introduction. This implies that we were not born in this state; but we are brought into it. "By whom we have access by faith"; by Christ as the author and principal agent; by faith as the means of this access. Not by Christ in consideration of any merit of ours; but in consideration of our believing dependence upon Him.

**B. The Saints' Happy Standing.** "Wherein we stand": a posture that denotes our discharge from guilt. It denotes also our progress. While we stand we are going; we must not lie down, as if we had already attained, but stand as those that are pressing forward. The phrase denotes, further, our perseverance. We stand firm and safe, upheld by God's power. It denotes our confirmation in God's favor.

## III. WE REJOICE IN THE HOPE OF THE GLORY OF GOD. Verse 2.

**A. The Persons who may Hope for the Future Glory of God.** Besides the happiness in hand there is a happiness in the hope of the glory which God will put upon His saints in heaven. Only those who have access by faith into the grace of God now may hope for the glory of God hereafter. There is no good hope of glory but what is founded in grace; grace is glory begun, the earnest and assurance of glory. He "will give grace and glory" (Psalm 84:11).

**B. The Future Hope of Glory is Sufficient for Present Joy.**
Those who hope for the glory of God hereafter have enough
to rejoice in now. It is the duty of those who hope for heaven
to rejoice in those hopes.

## IV. WE GLORY IN TRIBULATIONS FOR GOD. Verse 3.
One would think that the peace, grace, glory, and the joy in
the hope of it were more than we could pretend to have and
yet it is not only so, there are more instances of our happiness;
we glory in tribulations, especially tribulation for righteousness'
sake. Why?

**A. Tribulation Produces Patience.** Tribulation worketh patience, not in or of itself, but the powerful grace of God working
in and with the tribulation. It proves and by proving improves
patience; as parts and gifts increase by exercise. That which
works patience is a matter of joy; for patience does us more
good than tribulations can do us hurt. Tribulation in itself
works impatience; but as it is sanctified to the saints it works
patience.

**B. Patience Produces Experience.** It works an experience
of God which gives songs in the night. The patient sufferers
have the greatest experience of the divine consolations which
abound as afflictions abound. It is by tribulation that we make
an experiment of our own sincerity and therefore such tribulations are called trials. It works an approbation, as he is ap-
proved that has passed the test. Job's tribulation wrought
patience and that patience produced an approbation (Job 2:3).

**C. Experience Produces Hope.** He who, being thus tried,
comes forth as gold will thereby be encouraged to hope. This
experiment or approbation is not so much the ground as the
evidence of our hope and a special friend to it. Experience of
God is a prop to our hope; He who has delivered, does and
will deliver. Experience of ourselves helps to evidence our
sincerity.

**D. Hope Makes Not Ashamed.** It is a hope that will not
deceive us. Nothing confounds more than disappointment.

Everlasting shame and confusion will be caused by the perishing of the expectation of the wicked, but "the hope of the righteous shall be gladness" (Proverbs 10:28; see Psalms 22:5; 71:1). Or, it makes us unashamed of our sufferings. Since we have hopes of glory we are not ashamed of these sufferings.

## CONCLUSION

This hope will not disappoint us because it is sealed with the Holy Spirit as the Spirit of love. The love is shed abroad as sweet ointment perfuming the soul; as rain watering it and making it fruitful. The ground of all our comfort and holiness, and perseverance in both is laid in the shedding abroad of the love of God in our hearts. It is that which constrains us (II Corinthians 5:14).

# 26

# *The Holy Spirit and Prayer*

> *Likewise the Spirit also helpeth our infirm-
> ities: for we know not what we should pray
> for as we ought: but the Spirit itself maketh
> intercession for us with groanings which
> cannot be uttered. And He that searcheth
> the hearts knoweth what is the mind of the
> Spirit, because He maketh intercession for
> the saints according to the will of God.*
> —Romans 8:26-27

THE APOSTLE, having fully explained the doctrine of justification and pressed the necessity of sanctification, in this chapter applies himself to the consolation of the Lord's people. It is the will of God that His people should be a comforted people. And we have here such a display of the unspeakable privileges of true believers as may furnish us with an abundant matter for joy and peace in believing, that by all of these immutable things, in which it is impossible for God to lie, we might have a strong consolation. One of these privileges is prayer. While we are in this world, hoping and waiting for what we see not, we must be praying. Hope supposes desire and that desire offered up to God is prayer.

## I. THE NEED FOR THE AID OF THE HOLY SPIRIT IN PRAYER.

A. **We Do Not Know What to Pray for as We Ought.**
We are not competent judges of our own condition. We are short-sighted and very much biased in favor of the flesh and apt to separate the end from the way. "Ye know not what ye ask" (Matthew 20:22). We are like foolish children that are ready to cry for fruit before it is ripe (Luke 9:54-56).

1. *Because we are short-sighted.*

2. *Because we are biased in favor of the flesh.*

## B. We Do Not Know How to Pray as We Ought.

1. *Hindrances in prayer.* As to the manner, we know not how to pray as we ought. It is not enough that we do that which is good, but we must do it well; seek in a due order; and here we are often at a loss; graces are weak, affections cold, thoughts wandering. It is not always easy for one to find it in his heart to pray (II Samuel 7:27).

2. *Hindrances to prayer affect all believers.* The Apostle speaks of the matter of not knowing how to pray in the first person: "We know not." He puts himself among the rest. Folly, weakness, and distraction in prayer are that of which all the saints complain. If so great a saint as Paul knew not how to pray, what reason have we to go forth about that duty in our own strength?

## II. THE HOLY SPIRIT'S AID IN PRAYER.

### A. He Helps our Infirmities.

1. *The explanation.* He helps our praying infirmities which most easily beset us in that duty. The Spirit in the Word of God helps — many rules and promises are there for our help. The Spirit in the heart helps — dwelling in us, working in us, as the Spirit of grace and supplication; for this end the Holy Spirit was poured out.

2. *The requirement.* He helps us as we help one that would lift up a burden, by lifting at the other end; He helps with us, with us doing our endeavor, putting forth the strength we have. We must not sit still and expect that the Spirit will do all. We cannot without God and He will not without us.

## B. How He Helps our Infirmities.

1. *By dictating our requests.* The Spirit dictates our requests, indites our petitions, draws up our plea for us. He as an enlightening Spirit teaches us what to pray for; as a sanctifying Spirit He works and excites praying graces; as

a comforting Spirit He silences our fears and helps us over all of our discouragements. He is the spring of all our desires and breathings toward God.

2. *With unutterable groanings.* The strength and fervency of those desires which the Holy Spirit works are hereby intimated. There may be praying in the Spirit where there is not a word spoken; as Moses (Exodus 14:15) and Hannah (I Samuel 1:13) prayed. It is not the rhetoric and eloquence, but the faith and fervency of our prayers that the Spirit works, as an intercessor, in us.

3. *According to God's will.* The Spirit in the heart never contradicts the Spirit in the Word. Those desires that are contrary to the will of God do not come from the Spirit. The Spirit interceding in us evermore melts our wills into the will of God. "Not as I will but as Thou wilt."

## III. THE SUCCESS OF THE HOLY SPIRIT'S AID IN PRAYER.

A. **God Knows our Need.** This is assured because He searches the heart.

1. *This Divine heart searching is a disturbing truth to the hypocrite.* To the hypocrite, whose religion lies in his tongue, nothing is more dreadful than the fact that God searches the heart and sees through all of his disguises.

2. *This Divine heart searching is a comforting truth to the believer.* To a sincere Christian, who makes heart-work of his duty, nothing is more comfortable than the fact that God searches the heart, for then He will hear and answer those desires which we lack words to express. He knows "what we have need of before we ask" (Matthew 6:8).

B. **God Knows the Mind of the Spirit.** He knows what is the mind of His own Spirit in us. As He always hears the Son interceding for us (John 11:42), so He always hears the Spirit interceding in us, because His intercession is according to the will of God.

1. *He hears the intercession of Christ for us.*
2. *He hears the intercession of the Spirit in us.*

## CONCLUSION

What could have been done more for the comfort of the Lord's people? Christ has said, "Whatever you ask the Father according to His will, He will give it you." But how shall we learn to ask according to His will? The Spirit will teach us that. There it is, that the children of God never seek in vain.

**27**

# The Christian's Responsibility to God

> *I beseech you therefore, brethren, by the*
> *mercies of God, that ye present your bodies*
> *a living sacrifice, holy, acceptable unto*
> *God, which is your reasonable service.*
> *And be not conformed to this world: but*
> *be ye transformed by the renewing of your*
> *mind, that ye may prove what is that good,*
> *and acceptable, and perfect will of God.*
> —Romans 12:1-2

THE APOSTLE having confirmed the fundamental doctrines of Christianity now stresses Christian duties. Christianity is practical. It tends to the right ordering of the life. It is designed not only to inform our judgments, but to transform our lives. The text reminds us of our duty to God.

## I. THE PRESENTATION OF THE BODY TO GOD.

### A. The Nature of the Presentation.

1. *A voluntary sacrifice.* Presenting of them denotes a voluntary act done by virtue of that absolute despotic power which the will has over the body and all the members of it. It must be a free will offering. This is to glorify God with our bodies (I Corinthians 6:20).

2. *A living sacrifice.* A body sincerely devoted to God is a living sacrifice, a living sacrifice inspired with the spiritual life of the soul. It is Christ living in the soul by faith that makes the body a living sacrifice (Galatians 2:20). Holy love kindles the sacrifices, puts life into the duties.

3. *A holy sacrifice.* There must be real holiness which stands in an entire rectitude of heart and life, by which we are

114

conformed in both to the nature and will of God. Our bodies must not be made the instruments of sin and uncleanness, but set apart for God and put to holy uses.

## B. The Arguments Favoring the Presentation.

1. *The mercies of God.* God is a merciful God, therefore let us present our bodies to Him. He will be sure to use them kindly and knows how to consider the frames of them for He is of infinite compassion. We receive from Him every day the fruits of His mercy (Lamentations 3:22).

2. *The acceptability of it to God.* The great end to which we should labor is to be accepted of the Lord (II Corinthians 5:9), to have Him well pleased with our persons and performances. Now these living sacrifices are acceptable to God; while the sacrifices of the wicked, although fat and costly, are an abomination to the Lord.

3. *The reasonableness of the presentation.* God does not impose upon us anything hard or unreasonable, but that which is altogether agreeable to the principles of right reason. God deals with us as with rational creatures and will have us so to deal with Him. Thus must the body be presented to God.

## II. RENEWAL OF THE MIND.

## A. The Meaning of Renewal of the Mind. See to it that there
be a saving change wrought in you and that it be carried on. Conversion and sanctification are the renewing of the mind; a change not of substance, but of the qualities of the soul.

1. *Conversion.* It is the receiving of new dispositions, inclinations, sympathies, and antipathies; the understanding enlightened, the conscience softened, the thoughts rectified and the will bowed to the will of God; the affections made spiritual and heavenly: so that the man is not what he was (II Corinthians 5:17).

2. *Sanctification.* The progress of sanctification, dying to sin more and more and living to righteousness more and more,

is the carrying on of this renewing work until it is perfected in glory.

## B. The Manner of the Renewal of the Mind.

1. *It is the work of God.* We cannot work such a change ourselves; we could as soon make a new world as to make a new heart by any power of our own; it is God's work. It is God that turns us and then we are turned.

2. *It is our duty to seek God's grace to bring this about.* "Be ye transformed," that is, use the means which God has appointed and ordained for it. Lay your souls under the changing, transforming influences of the blessed Spirit; seek unto God for grace in the use of all the means of grace. Although the new man is created of God, yet we must put it on (Ephesians 4:24).

## C. The Obstacle to the Renewing of the Mind.

1. *The obstacle named.* The great enemy to this renewing which we must avoid is conformity to this world. All the disciples and followers of the Lord Jesus must be nonconformists to this world. Do not fashion yourselves according to the world.

2. *The obstacle explained.* We must not conform to the things of the world; they are mutable and the fashion of them is passing away. Do not conform to the lusts of the flesh or the lusts of the eye. We must not conform to the men of the world, of that which lies in wickedness, that is, we must not follow the multitude to do evil.

## D. The Effect of the Renewal of the Mind. It is the proving of the good, acceptable, and perfect revealed will of God concerning what He requires of us. This reminds us of three things.

1. *The will of God is good, acceptable, and perfect.* It is good in itself; it is good for us. It is acceptable, it is pleasing to God. It is perfect, to which nothing can be added. The revealed will of God is a sufficient rule of faith and practice.

2. *The will of God should be proved.* It concerns the Christian to know the will of God; to know it with judgment and approbation; to know it experimentally; to know the excellency of the will of God by the experience of a conformity to it.

3. *The transformed mind is the best able to prove the will of God.* The promise is, "If any man will do His will, he shall know of the doctrine" (John 7:17). An honest, humble heart that has spiritual senses exercised and is delivered into the mold of the Word, loves it and practices it.

## CONCLUSION

Our duty to God, as Christians, is to yield to Him and transform our minds by His grace. Thus to be godly is to surrender ourselves to God. This is a prerequisite to fruitful service.

**28**

## The Treasure in Earthen Vessels

> *But we have this treasure in earthen vessels, that the excellency of the power may be of God and not of us.*
>
> —II Corinthians 4:7

THE heavens indeed declare the glory of God, but they do not show us how we may glorify God, much less how we may be glorified with Him. Here, therefore, where natural reason and natural religion leave us at a loss, the Gospel of Christ takes us up and shows us the glory of God shining in the face of Christ, where it shines clearer and stronger and brighter and with more satisfaction than it does in the face of the whole creation; for it declares Christ reconciling the world to Himself.

### I. THE GOSPEL OF CHRIST IS THE TREASURE.

**A. The Gospel is a Treasure because it Consists of an Abundance of That which is of Inestimable Value.** There are treasures of wisdom and knowledge in the truths which the Gospel reveals to us, about which the understanding finds the best employment. There are treasures of comfort and joy in the offers which the Gospel makes to us and the blessings it assures to all believers, in which not only the necessities of the soul are well provided for, but its desires abundantly satisfied and its true and lasting happiness inviolably secured. There is a treasure of grace and strength in the Spirit and His operations in us.

**B. The Gospel is a Treasure because there is no End to It.** It is deposited in good hands whence we may draw from it, but cannot be deprived of it. It is deposited in the wisdom and counsel of God, in Christ, in the Scriptures. It is a treasure that will not only suit the present exigences of the soul, but will last as long as it lasts. It is the word of the Lord which endures forever, when all the glory of man is withered as the grass. It is a treasure which glorified saints will be living plentifully and pleasantly upon to eternity.

**C. The Gospel is a Treasure because it is of Universal Use.** It is not only valuable in itself, but every way suitable and serviceable to us. It is a treasure of food for all those who hunger and thirst after righteousness. It is a treasure of arms and ammunition for our spiritual warfare. It furnishes us with the answers to every temptation and with the whole armor of God. It is a treasure in the heart of every true believer. If the gospel of Christ has the innermost and uppermost place in our lives we are rich toward God.

## II. CHRISTIANS ARE THE EARTHEN VESSELS.

**A. They Are Only Vessels.** They can give only what they have received. God is the fountain of light and life and living waters and all their springs are in Him. It is the commandment which is the lamp and the law is the light; the believers are but as candlesticks in which this light is set up and by which it is held forth. A man can receive nothing which he can depend upon himself or recommend to others with any assurance, unless it be given him from above.

**B. They Are Earthen Vessels.** Believers are compared to earthen vessels because: (1) They are made of the same mold as other people; (2) oftentimes in respect to their outward condition they are of small account, men of low degree; (3) they are subject to many infirmities; (4) not all of the same constitution — some are weak and others are strong; (5) they are what God, the Potter, makes them; (6) they are vessels of service; (7) oftentimes despised and trampled upon by men; (8) they are frail and mortal and dying and on that account earthen vessels.

## III. GOD PLACES THE TREASURE IN EARTHEN VESSELS TO MAGNIFY HIS POWER.

**A. Divine Power was Given to the Apostles to Strengthen Them for their Work.** To preach down Judaism and paganism and preach up the kingdom of the crucified Jesus was a service that required a far greater strength, both of judgment and resolution, than the apostles had of themselves. If they had not been full of power by the Spirit of the Lord they could never have spoken as they did with that wisdom which all their adversaries were not able to gainsay or resist; could never have made such vigorous attacks upon the devil's kingdom, nor have gathered such a harvest of souls to Jesus Christ.

**B. Divine Power was Given to the Apostles to Support Them in their Hardships.** God chose the service of such men as were despised in order that He might magnify His own power in keeping the spirit which He had made from failing before Him. One would wonder how the apostles kept up their spirits. It was not by any power of their own, but underneath them were the everlasting arms and when they were pressed out of measure, above strength, so that they despaired of life, yet they did not faint because they were borne up by the power of God who raises the dead.

**C. Divine Power was Given to the Apostles to Give Them Success.** The world was to be enlightened with the lights and enriched with the treasure that was lodged in the earthen vessels. It is not what the apostles have wrought, but what God has wrought by them. The Gospel of Christ is the power of God to salvation. The wonderful achievements of the Gospel! The trophies of its victory over the powers of darkness! The numerous instances of its convincing and sanctifying power! Many sinful hearts have by it been made to tremble and many gracious souls to triumph.

## CONCLUSION

Thank God for the Gospel treasure though it is in earthen vessels. Thank God that it is in such vessels that it may be the nearer to you and the more within your reach. Give all diligence to make sure your interest in this treasure. What will it avail us that we have the Gospel in our land if we have it not in our hearts? What will it avail us that we have the sound of it about us and not the savor of it within us?

**29**

# The Promises of God

*Having therefore these promises, dearly
beloved, let us cleanse ourselves from all
filthiness of the flesh and spirit, perfecting
holiness in the fear of God.*
—II Corinthians 7:1

WE WILL consider the promises of God under four
heads, namely, the Christian's possession of the promises, the content of the promises, the blessed fruits of the promises, and the
Christian's obligation or duty because of the promises.

## I. THE POSSESSION OF GOD'S PROMISES.

**A. The Privilege of the Possession of the Promises.** It is
the unspeakable privilege of all believers to have as a certain
possession the precious promises of God.

**B. The Explanation of the Possession of the Promises.** We
have the promises as tokens of God's favor towards us; as
fruits of Christ's purchase; as declarations of God's good will
toward men; as a foundation of our faith and hope; as the directions and encouragements of our desires in prayer; as the means
by which the grace of God works for our holiness and comfort,
as the earnest and assurance of future blessedness.

## II. THE CONTENT OF GOD'S PROMISES.

**A. Promises of Spiritual Blessings.** God has promised that
all of our sins shall be pardoned (Isaiah 43:25); that He will
answer our prayers (John 14:13); that He will silence our
fears (Isaiah 41:13); that He will proportion our trials to our
strength (I Corinthians 10:13); that He will perfect the work

122

of grace in us (Philippians 1:6); that He will never desert
us (Hebrews 13:5); that He will give us victory over our
spiritual enemies (Romans 16:20).

B. **Promises of Physical Blessings.** He has also promised
to protect us from all evil (Psalm 121:7, 8); to feed us with
food convenient for us (Psalm 37:3); to raise up our bodies
to life again (John 6:40).

## III. THE FRUITS OF GOD'S PROMISES.

A. **Strength.** The promises furnish us with a strength sufficient against sin and for duty.

B. **Victory.** These promises speak the language of Caleb
and Joshua who said, "We are well able to overcome the
people," when they were about to enter into Canaan while
the other spies discouraged the tribes of Israel. Thus we may
say through the strength of divine grace we shall be enabled
to overcome all of our spiritual enemies, namely, the world,
the flesh, and the devil.

C. **Faithfulness.** God is faithful to the promises which He
has made to us. Therefore, we must not be false to those
promises which we have made to Him.

D. **Obedience.** In having these promises we have great honor
put upon us and we ought to carry it as becomes us. God
has promised to be to us a faithful God, a loving and tender
Father. Let us not wander out of the way of duty.

E. **Reward.** The promises secure to us an abundant reward
for our obedience. "Therefore, my beloved brethren, be ye
steadfast, unmovable, always abounding in the work of the
Lord, forasmuch as ye know that your labor is not in vain in
the Lord" (I Corinthians 15:58).

## IV. THE CHRISTIAN'S DUTY IN VIEW OF GOD'S PROMISES.

A. **To be Cleansed from all Filthiness of the Flesh and Spirit.**

1. *The Reason.* Look upon sin as filthiness. It is odious to
God, contrary to that purity of nature which appears in His

promises. Look upon sin as that which unfits us for communion with God. Sin in Scripture is called and compared
to a wound, to a plague, to leprosy.

2. *The manner.* Let us cleanse ourselves from this filthiness
by receiving the Lord Jesus Christ; for it is He who is
made to us both righteousness and sanctification. Let us
mortify the habits of sin and purge out the old leaven, both
in the head and in the heart. Let us watch against all
occasions of sin. Keep at a distance from everything which
has the appearance of evil. Let us resolve for the future to
have no more to do with sin.

3. *The extent.* (a) We must cleanse ourselves from all filthiness of the flesh — slothfulness and the love of ease, sensuality and the love of pleasure, from gratifying the desires of
the body with forbidden fruit. (b) We must cleanse ourselves from all filthiness of the spirit — pride, covetousness,
love of the world, fraud, deceit, injustice, sinful anger,
malice, hatred, and desire of revenge.

## B. To Perfect Holiness in the Fear of God.

1. *The necessity for holiness.* We cannot perfect holiness unless we begin it. This means that we must be devoted to
God, conformed to His likeness and to His will, employed
in the worship of God, engaged in the interests of God's
work amongst men. To be holy is to be on the Lord's
side and to espouse His cause, to be His witnesses, to
be courageous and valiant for the truth, to contend earn-
estly for it.

2. *The necessity of sincerity in holiness.* We must be sincere
in our holiness, that is perfecting holiness. For sincerity
is our gospel perfection, as a good man said. By this is
understood that (a) the whole man must be sanctified. The
understanding must be enlightened, the will brought into
obedience to the will of God, both to the will of His precepts to do them and to do the will of His providences to submit to them. (b) The whole work of God must be regarded
and respected (Psalm 119:6, 80, 128).

3. *The necessity of progress in holiness.* (a) The habits of grace must grow more confirmed and rooted, our resolutions against sin more settled and our resolutions for God and duty more steady. (b) The actings of grace must grow more vigorous and lively. (c) We must be more watchful and on our guard. (d) We must be actuated and animated by the fear of God resulting in faithfulness in family and private devotions, a reverent regard for the majesty and authority of God, and fear of God's wrath and displeasure.

## CONCLUSION

Apply the promises to yourselves, live upon them, take them to be your heritage forever. Both you that are young and you that are old treasure up the promises. Apply the precepts to yourselves and live up to them and be holy in all manner of conduct. Keep a conscience always void of offence both towards God and towards man.

# 30

## Christian Unity

*Endeavoring to keep the unity of the Spirit
in the bond of peace.*      —Ephesians 4:3

THE FORMER part of this epistle (chapters 1-3) consists of several important doctrinal truths. The latter part (chapters 4-6) contains the most weighty and serious exhortations that can be given. The former part informs the minds of men in the great doctrines of the gospel and the latter is designed for the direction of their lives. The text exhorts to mutual unity and concord.

## I. THE MEANS OF CHRISTIAN UNITY.

### A. The Statement of the Means. See verse 2.

1. *Lowliness and meekness.* By lowliness we are to understand humility, and entertaining mean thoughts of ourselves, which is opposed to pride. By meekness is meant that excellent disposition of soul which makes men unwilling to provoke others and not easily to be provoked or offended with their infirmities. It is opposed to angry resentments and peevishness.

2. *Longsuffering and loving forbearance.* Longsuffering implies a patient bearing of injuries without seeking revenge. Forbearing one another in love signifies bearing their infirmities out of a principle of love; and so as not to cease to love them on the account of these.

### B. The Importance of the Means.

1. *These are necessary because of the perversity of human nature.* The best Christians have need to bear one with another and to make the best one of another; to provoke

one another's graces (Hebrews 10:24), and not their passions. We find much in ourselves which is hard to forgive ourselves; and therefore, we must not think it much if we find that in others which we think hard to forgive them; and yet we must forgive them as we forgive ourselves.

2. *These are necessary for the practice of unity.* The first step toward unity is humility; without this there will be no meekness, no patience, no forbearance; and without these, no unity. Pride and passion break the peace and make all the mischief. Humility and meekness restore the peace and keep it. Only by pride comes contention (Proverbs 13:10); only by humility comes love. The more lowly-mindedness, the more like-mindedness. We do not walk worthy of the vocation wherewith we are called if we are not meek and lowly of heart.

## II. THE NATURE OF CHRISTIAN UNITY.

### A. It is a Spiritual Unity.

1. *The seat of Christian unity.* The seat of Christian unity is in the heart or spirit; it does not lie in one set of thoughts or in one form and mode of worship, but in one heart and one soul.

2. *The producer of Christian unity.* This unity of heart and affection is of the Spirit of God; it is wrought by Him and is one of the fruits of the Spirit. This we should endeavor to keep. We must do our utmost. If others quarrel with us we must take all possible care not to quarrel with them. If others will despise and hate us we must not despise and hate them.

### B. It is a Peaceful Unity.

1. *The bond of peace unites persons.* Peace is a bond which unites persons and makes them live friendly one with another. A peaceable disposition and conduct bind Christians together; whereas discord and quarrel disband and disunite their hearts and affections.

2. *The bond of peace strengthens society.* The bond of peace is the strength of society. Not that it can be imagined that all good people should be in everything of the same senti-

ments and the same judgment; but the bond of peace unites them all together so that they will not be unnecessarily obstinate one to another. As in a bundle of rods, they may be of different lengths and different strength; but when they are tied together by one band, they are much stronger than any, even than the thickest and strongest were of themselves.

## III. THE MOTIVES FOR THE PROMOTION OF CHRISTIAN UNITY.

### A. The Consideration of the Various Unities.

1. *The enumeration of the unities.* One body and one Spirit; one hope (verse 4). One Lord; one faith; one baptism (verse 5). One God and Father of all (verse 6).

2. *The significance of the various unities.* There should be one heart because there is one body and one Spirit. Two hearts in one body would be monstrous. The one body is animated by one Spirit, the Holy Spirit. All Christians are called to the same hope and therefore should be of one heart. All Christians have the same Lord to whom they are subject and were saved by the same faith. All were baptized by the same baptism in the name of the Father, Son, and Holy Spirit. One God owns all of the true members of the church for His children.

### B. The Consideration of the Various Gifts.

1. *The freely bestowed gifts.* "But unto every one of us (Christians) is given grace, according to the measure of the gift of Christ" (verse 7). Every Christian has received some gift of grace, in some kind or degree or other, for the mutual help of one another. All of the members of Christ owe all the gifts and graces that they have to Him: and this is a good reason why we should love one another because to "every one of us is given grace." All to whom Christ has given grace and upon whom He bestowed His gifts ought to love one another.

2. *The design of the bestowal of the gifts.* The gifts of Christ were intended for the good of His church and in order to

advance His cause and interest among men. All these being designed for one common end, is a good reason why all Christians should agree in brotherly love; and not envy one another's gifts. All of the gifts are for the restoration, strengthening, and confirmation of the saints so that they might contribute to the good of the whole.

## CONCLUSION

Christians ought to accommodate themselves to the Gospel by which they are called and to the glory to which they are called. We are called Christians; we must answer that name, and live like Christians. We are called to God's kingdom and glory; that kingdom and glory, therefore, we must mind and walk as becomes the heirs of them. Therefore, we should put forth every effort "to keep the unity of the Spirit in the bond of peace."

# 31

# *The Instruction of Youth*

> *Hold fast the form of sound words which thou hast heard of me in faith and love which is in Christ Jesus.*
>
> —II Timothy 1:13

TIMOTHY was blessed with two advantages in his childhood and youth; he was brought up under the tutoring of a godly mother and grandmother (II Timothy 1:5; 3:15) and under the instruction of a faithful ministry (II Timothy 1:13).

## I. THE ADVANTAGE TO YOUTH TO LEARN GOD'S WORD.

### A. The Words of the Gospel are Sound Words.

1. *This implies that they are valuable and valid.* They are what they seem to be. You may trust them as you may that which is sound and will never be made ashamed of your confidence in them. They are unchangeable and inviolable.

2. *This implies that there is virtue to be drawn from them.* The word translated *sound* is sometimes rendered *healthful* or *healing.* These words when mixed with faith restore the soul and heal its maladies.

### B. The Words of the Gospel when Simply Systematized are Helpful. It is good to have forms of the sound words drawn up for the use of learners. These should not take the place of the Scriptures, but a help to the further study of them.

1. *By this the main principles of Christianity are brought together.* Catechisms and confessions of faith pick up from

130

the several parts of Holy Writ those passages which contain the essentials of religion, the foundations and main pillars upon which Christianity is built.

2. *By this the truths of God are arranged and put in order.* These forms of sound words show us the order that is in God's Word, the harmony of divine truths, how one thing tends to another and all center in Christ.

3. *By this the truths of God are brought down to the understanding of youth.* To those who are young, the Scriptures need to be explained; to them we must give the sense and cause them to understand the reading and this is done in part by these forms of sound words.

C. The Words of the Gospel when Well Taught and Learned Bring Blessing.

1. *The time spent in learning God's Word is well employed.* If the time is spent in good exercises, in conversing with the Word of God, in reviewing and repeating to ourselves the things of God it is better than keeping a man from wasting an estate.

2. *It gives ability to better understand and profit by the Word preached.* Those who have not been taught do most need instruction by the preaching of the Word, yet those who have been well taught do most desire it because they understand it.

3. *It gives a good foundation for the work of grace in the soul.* Ordinarily Christ enlightens the understanding by the use of means and gives a knowledge of divine things by the instructions of parents and ministers and afterwards by His Spirit and grace brings them home to the mind and conscience resulting in salvation.

4. *It arms against the assaults and insinuations of seducers.* Those who are well instructed in the Scriptures and understand the evidence of divine truths are aware of the fallacies with which others are beguiled and know how to detect and escape them.

5. *It prepares one to do good to others.* Your being well instructed in the forms of sound words will qualify you to be useful in your generation for the glory of God and the edification of others.

6. *It assists the spiritual progress of the believer.* Timothy by the help of these forms of sound words, was nourished up in faith and good doctrine (I Timothy 4:6). They who have pure hearts and clean hands hereby shall become stronger.

## II. THE CHARGE TO HOLD FAST GOD'S WORD.

### A. To Hold Fast in Remembrance.

1. *It will be of good use.* It will be of good use to you to retain the words you learn; and in order to do that frequently review them and repeat them over to yourselves.

2. *It will be ready for use.* The remembrance of them will be of use to us daily; both to fortify us against every evil word and work and to furnish us for every good word and work.

### B. To Hold Fast in Faith.

1. *Assent to the words as faithful sayings.* You must set your seal that God is true and every word of His is so, even that which you cannot comprehend as the eternity of God or the immensity of His perfections.

2. *Grow to a full assurance of the truth.* Know not only what it is we believe; but why we believe it; and be ready always to give a reason of the hope that is in us (I Peter 3:15).

3. *Faithful application of the truth.* You must make faithful application of these sound and healing words to yourselves; else they will not answer the end or be healing to you any more than uneaten food.

### C. To Hold Fast in Love.

1. *Delight in them.* Take delight in them and in the knowledge of them. That which we love we will hold fast and not easily part with it. That which is not thus delighted in will not be long held fast.

2. *Be affected by them.* Lay them to heart as things that concern you to the last degree. Be affected with love to the Word of God and then you will conceive a high value and veneration for Christ.

3. *Be influenced by them.* As faith works by love, so love works by keeping God's commandments (I John 5:3). We then hold fast the sayings of Christ when we govern ourselves by them.

B. **To Hold Fast in Christ Jesus.** We must hold fast the sound words of the Gospel in that faith and love which has:

1. *Christ as the author.* It is that faith and love which is wrought in us, not by our own strength or resolutions, but by the Spirit and grace of Christ.

2. *Christ as the object.* It is Christ that we must embrace and hold fast. It is by faith in Christ and love to Christ that we must hold fast what we have received.

3. *Christ as the end.* It must be that faith and love which has an eye to Christ; which has this always in view, to glorify Christ and to be glorified with Christ.

## CONCLUSION

Let us close with a few words of exhortation. Let us bless God that our lot is cast in a land of light. Let parents faithfully instruct their children in the form of sound words. Let the ministers of Christ look upon themselves as under a charge to feed Christ's lambs.

# 32

# *The Faith of Abraham*

> *By faith Abraham obeyed. By faith he sojourned in the land of promise; for he looked for a city whose builder and maker is God. By faith Abraham offered up Isaac: accounting that God was able to raise him from the dead.*
> —Hebrews 11:8-10, 17-19

THE WRITER having, in the close of the foregoing chapter, recommended the grace of faith and a life of faith as the best preservative against apostacy; he now enlarges upon this excellent grace. In doing this he writes more about the achievements of Abraham's faith than any of the other patriarchs.

## I. THE GROUND OF ABRAHAM'S FAITH (verse 8).

### A. The Call of God.

1. *The nature of the call.* In Acts 7:2 Stephen relates the manner in which Abraham was called. This was an effectual call by which he was converted from the idolatry of his father's house. It was the call of God and therefore a sufficient ground for faith and rule of obedience.

2. *The lessons from the call.* (a) The grace of God is free in taking of the worst of men and making them the best. (b) God must come to us before we come to him. (c) In converting sinners God works a glorious work. (d) This call is to leave sin and sinful company.

### B. The Promise of God.

1. *The substance of the promise.* God promised Abraham that the place he was called to he would afterward receive for an inheritance.

2. *The observations concerning the promise.* God calls His people to an inheritance: by His effectual call He makes them children and so heirs. This inheritance is not immediately possessed by them, they must wait some time for it. However, the promise is sure and shall have its seasonable accomplishment. The faith of parents often procures blessings for their posterity.

## II. THE EXERCISE OF ABRAHAM'S FAITH (verses 8, 9, 17).

### A. An Implicit Obedience to the Call of God.

1. *He went out, not knowing where he went.* He placed himself in the hand of God to send him wherever He pleased. He subscribed to God's wisdom as best to direct; and submitted to His will as best to determine everything that concerned him. Implicit faith and obedience are due to God and to Him only.

2. *He sojourned in the land as a stranger.* This was in exercise of his faith. Abraham lived in Canaan as a sojourner, a stranger, and dwelt in tents with Isaac and Jacob. He lived there in an ambulatory moving condition, living in daily readiness for his removal. Thus should we all live in this world.

### B. An Implicit Obedience to the Command of God.

1. *It was a test of faith.* Genesis 22:1 tells us: "God in this tempted Abraham"; not to sin, for so God tempts no man (James 1:13), but tried his faith and obedience. God had before this tried the faith of Abraham; but this trial was greater than all. Read the account of it in Genesis 22.

2. *It was a test faithfully met.* Abraham obeyed; he offered up Isaac. He intentionally gave him up by his submissive soul to God and was ready to do it actually according to the command of God. He went as far in it as to the very critical moment when God prevented him.

## III. THE SUPPORTS OF ABRAHAM'S FAITH (verses 10, 19).

### A. The Hope of Heaven.

1. *The description of heaven.* It is a city; a regularly established, defended, and supplied society. It is a city with foundations: the unchangeable purposes and almighty power of God; the merits and mediation of the Lord Jesus; the promises of the everlasting covenant. It is a city which God planned and made.

2. *The influence of heaven.* He looked for it; he believed there was such a state; he waited for it. As he did so it was a support to him under all the trials of his sojourning; it helped him to bear patiently all the inconveniences of it and actively to discharge all the duties of it.

### B. The Power of God.

1. *He believed God could raise the dead.* His faith was supported by the sense he had of the mighty power of God, who was able to raise the dead; he reasoned thus with himself and so he resolved all his doubts.

2. *He believed God could raise his son from the dead.* It does not appear that Abraham had any expectation of being prevented from offering up his son; but he knew that God was able to raise him from the dead; and he believed that God would do so since such great things depended on his son which must fail if Isaac had not a further life.

## IV. THE REWARD OF ABRAHAM'S FAITH (verse 19).

### A. He Received His Son.
He had parted with him to God and God gave him back again. The best way to enjoy our comforts with comfort is to resign them up to God; He will then return them, if not in kind yet in kindness.

1. *Abraham had given his son to God.*

2. *God gave him back to Abraham.*

### B. He Received His Son from the Dead in a Figure.

1. *Abraham considered Isaac as dead.* He received him from the dead, for he gave him up for dead. He was as a dead

child to Abraham and the return was to him no less than a resurrection.

2. *This was a figure of the death and resurrection of Christ.* It was a figure or parable of the sacrifice and resurrection of Christ, of whom Isaac was a type. It was a figure and earnest of the glorious resurrection of all true believers whose life is not lost but hid with Christ in God (Colossians 3:3).

## CONCLUSION

Since the Gospel is the end and perfection of the Old Testament, which had no excellency except in its reference to Christ and the Gospel, it was expected that the faith of the New Testament saints should be as much more perfect than the faith of the Old Testament saints. Thus it should be with us.

# 33

## God, the Father and Fountain of All Good

> *Every good gift and every perfect gift is from above, and cometh down from the Father of lights, with whom is no variableness, neither shadow of turning. Of His own will begat He us with the Word of Truth, that we should be a kind of first-fruits of His creatures.* —James 1:17-18

AFTER the inscription and salutation (James 1:1), Christians are taught how to conduct themselves when under the cross. Several graces and duties are recommended; and those who endure their trials and afflictions as the apostle here directs, are pronounced blessed, and are assured of a glorious reward (verses 2-12). But those sins which bring sufferings, or the weaknesses and faults men are changeable with under them, are by no means to be imputed to God; who cannot be the author of sin, but is the author of all good.

## I. GOD IS THE FATHER OF LIGHTS.

A. **He is the Creator of Visible Light.** The visible light of the sun and of the heavenly bodies is from God. He said "Let there be light, and there was light" (Genesis 1:3). Thus God is at once represented as the Creator of the sun.

B. **He is Compared with Light.** "As the sun is the same in its nature and influences, though the earth and clouds oft interposing make it seem to us as varying, by its rising and setting, and by its different appearances or entire withdrawal; when the change is not in it: so God is unchangeable and our changes and shadows are not from any mutability or shadowy alterations in Him, but from ourselves" (Baxter). "The

Father of lights, *with whom there is no variableness, neither shadow of turning."* What the sun is in nature, God is in grace, providence, and glory; aye, and infinitely more.

## II. GOD IS THE GIVER OF EVERY GOOD GIFT.

**A. The Light that God Gives to Men.** As the Father of lights, God gives the light of reason. "The inspiration of the Almighty giveth understanding" (Job 32:8). He gives also the light of learning. Solomon's wisdom in the knowledge of nature, in the acts of government, and in all of his improvements is ascribed to God. The light of divine revelation is more immediately from above. The light of faith, purity, and all manner of consolation is from Him. So that we have nothing good except what we receive from God.

**B. The Acknowledgement that Men should Recognize.** We must own God as the author of all the powers and perfections that are in man and the giver of all the benefits which we have in and by those powers and perfections; but none of their darkness, their imperfections, or their ill actions are to be charged on the Father of lights; from Him proceeds every good and perfect gift, both pertaining to this life and that which is to come.

## III. GOD IS THE SOURCE OF REGENERATION AND ITS CONSEQUENCES.

**A. A True Christian is a Regenerated Person.** As every good gift is from God, so particularly our regeneration and all the holy, happy consequences which flow from it must be ascribed to Him. "Of His own will begat He us with the Word of Truth." A true Christian is a creature begotten anew. He becomes as different a person from what he was before the renewing influences of divine grace as if he were formed over again and born afresh, as is true of every true Christian.

**B. The Source of Regeneration.** The source of this good work is declared in the text. It is God's own will, not by our skill or power, not from any good foreseen in us or done by us, but purely from the good will and grace of God.

**C. The Means whereby Regeneration is Effected.** The means whereby this is effected is pointed out: "the Word of Truth," that is, the Gospel; as St. Paul expresses it more plainly, "I have begotten you in Jesus Christ through the gospel" (I Corinthians 4:15). This gospel is indeed a word of truth; or else it could never produce such real, such lasting, such great and noble effects. We may rely upon it and venture our immortal souls upon it. And we shall find it a means of our sanctification as it is a work of truth (John 17:17).

**D. The End and Design of Regeneration.** The end and design of God's giving renewing grace is here laid down; "that we should be a kind of first-fruits of His creatures"; that we should be God's portion and treasure and a more peculiar property to him, as the first-fruits were; and that we should become holy to the Lord, as the first-fruits were consecrated to Him. Christ is the First-fruits of Christians, Christians are the first-fruits of creatures.

## CONCLUSION

Thus we see that God is the Father and fountain of all good. We should take particular care not to err in our conceptions of God. Do not wander from the Word of God and accounts of Him you have there. Do not stray into erroneous opinions and go off from the standard of truth; the things which you have received from the Lord Jesus and by the direction of His Spirit. The truth, as it is in Jesus, stands thus: that God is not and cannot be the author and patronizer of anything that is evil; but must be acknowledged as the Cause and Spring of everything that is good. "Every good gift and every perfect gift is from above, and cometh down from the Father of lights, with whom is no variableness, neither shadow of turning."

# 34

# The Frailty and Hope of Man

> *All flesh is as grass, and all the glory of man as the flower of grass. The grass withereth, and the flower thereof falleth away: but the word of the Lord endureth forever.*        —I Peter 1:24, 25

In THE PLACE from which Peter quotes the text (Isaiah 40:6-8) it is a voice of one crying in the wilderness, who, that he might prepare the way of the Lord in the desert, is ordered to proclaim these words. I need not tell you that John the Baptist was that voice. It is his modest testimony concerning himself. These words set before us the vanity of the natural man and the enduring character of the holy Word of God: "All flesh is as grass; the Word of the Lord endureth forever."

## I. THE LAMENTATION: THE VANITY OF MAN.

### A. Man is Weak and Low.

1. *He is as lowly as the grass.* Mankind is indeed as numerous as the grass of the field, which multiplies, replenishes, and covers the earth; but like grass is of the earth, earthy, mean and of small account. Alas! the kingdoms of men which make so great a noise, so great a figure in this world, are as but so many fields of grass compared with the holy and blessed inhabitants of the upper regions.

2. *He is as weak as the grass.* Proud men think themselves like the strong and stately cedars, oaks, or pines, but they soon find themselves as grass, as grass of the field, liable to be nipt with every frost, trampled by every foot, continually insulted by common calamities of human life, which

we can no more resist or guard ourselves against than the grass can secure itself from the fatal blast, when the wind passeth over it and it is gone.

## B. Man is Withering and Fading.

1. *Therefore let us consider ourselves as grass.* Be not proud or presumptuous, be not confident of a long continuance here. We must expect to wither and should prepare accordingly and lay up our portion and happiness in none of the delights and accommodations of this life, but in something suited to the nature of an immortal soul. We may wither suddenly and know not how soon; therefore we must never adjourn to another day the necessary preparations for our removal. Let us not indulge the body too much nor bestow too much time, care, and pains upon it to the neglect of the soul.

2. *Therefore let us consider others as grass.* Let us see others also to be as grass and cease from men, because mankind is no more than thus to be accounted. If all flesh is grass, then let us not trust in the arm of flesh, for it will soon be a withered arm and unable to support and protect us. They who make it their arm will be like the heath in the desert, destitute and dejected. Grass is too short, too slender to lean upon.

## II. THE CONSOLATION: THE ETERNAL WORD OF GOD.

## A. The Bible is Everlasting Truth.

1. *It saves.* Though man and his glory are fading and withering, yet God and His Word are everliving and everlasting. Nothing can make man a solid, substantial being except the new birth; being born again of the incorruptible seed which is the Word of God. This will transform him into a most excellent creature, whose glory will not fade like a flower,

but shine like an angel.   This word is daily set before us
in the preaching of the Gospel.

2. *It preserves.*   The only way to render this perishing creature
incorruptible is to receive the Word of God, for that remains
everlasting truth and if received will preserve him to everlasting life and abide with him forever.

B. **The Bible is an Everlasting Rule of Faith and Practice.**
You profess to make the Scripture the commanding rule of
your worship and you say that you cannot admit any religious
rites but what are there appointed; but you contradict yourselves and give the lie to your profession if you do not make
the Scriptures the commanding rule of your conduct also.
Govern your thoughts, words, and actions by the Word of God
and not by the will of the flesh or the course of this world.   As
Christianity is found in our Bibles, so our Bibles should be
found in our hearts and lives.

1. *It is the rule of our worship.*

2. *It should be the rule of our life.*

C. **The Bible is an Everlasting Fountain of Comfort.**

1. *It refreshes and encourages.*   There is in the Word of the
Lord an everlasting fountain of comfort and consolation for
us to be refreshed and encouraged thereby and to draw
water from it with joy.   Study your Bibles.   Let God's
Word be your delight and your counsellor, make it familiar
to you and when you go it shall lead you, when you sleep
it shall keep you, when you wake it shall talk with you.
Take God's statutes as your heritage forever and let them
be the rejoicing of your hearts.

2. *It is the foundation of our hopes.*   God's Word is an everlasting foundation on which to build our hopes.   The
foundation of God stands sure (II Timothy 2:19).   This
never-failing Word is the firm and immoveable rock upon
which the church is built, therefore the gates of hell shall
not prevail against it.

## CONCLUSION

Man in his utmost glory is still a withering, fading, dying creature. In his entrance into the world, in his life, and in his fall he is like grass. Take him in all of his glory; his wit, beauty, strength, vigor, wealth, honor; these are but as the flower of grass which soon withers and dies away. Divine revelation will ride out the storm of all opposition and triumph over the powers of darkness. It will not only keep its ground, but gain its point. It goes forth conquering and to conquer.

# 35

# *Meekness and Quietness of Spirit*

> *Even the ornament of a meek and quiet spirit, which is in the sight of God of great price.*          —I Peter 3:4

THE Apostle Peter endeavors to wean the Christians from the vanity of outward ornaments and to bring them into love with the better ornaments, those of the mind, the graces of the blessed Spirit, called "the hidden man of the heart"; one of which is meekness and quietness of spirit.

## I. THE NATURE OF MEEKNESS AND QUIETNESS OF SPIRIT.

Meekness and quietness seem to import much the same thing, but the latter having something of metaphor in it illustrates the former.

### A. The Explanation of the Character of Meekness.

1. *The relation to God.*  It is the easy and quiet submission of the soul to the word and providence of God, to His whole will.

2. *In relation to man.*  This Holy Spirit wrought fruit teaches us to prudently govern our own anger and teaches and enables us patiently to bear the anger of others.

### B. The Character of Quietness.
1. *What it is.*  Quietness is the evenness, the composure, and the rest of the soul, which speaks both of the nature and the excellency of the grace of meekness.  The greatest comfort and happiness of man is sometimes set forth by quietness.

145

2. *How it illustrates meekness.* (a) We must be quiet as the air is quiet from the winds. (b) As the sea is quiet from the waves. Uneasiness of man quieted. (c) Quiet as the land is quiet from war. Quietness of soul. (d) The quietness of a weaned child, satisfied.

## II. THE EXCELLENCY OF MEEKNESS AND QUIETNESS OF SPIRIT.

### A. The Power of a Meek and Quiet Spirit.

1. *It gives victory.* No triumphant chariot is so easy, safe, and glorious as that in which a meek and quiet soul rides over all the provocations of an injurious world. Meekness is a victory over ourselves and the rebellious lusts in our bosoms.

2. *It gives beauty.* The beauty of a thing consists in the symmetry, harmony, and agreeableness of all parts. What is meekness, but the soul's agreement with itself? Next to the beauty of holiness, which is the soul's agreement with God, is the beauty of meekness.

3. *It is an ornament.* The text speaks of it as an adorning much more excellent and valuable than gold, pearls, or the most costly array. It is an adorning of the soul which recommends us to God. It is an adorning of God's making and accepting.

4. *It gives true courage.* True courage is such a presence of mind as enables a man rather to suffer than to sin; to choose affliction rather than iniquity; to pass by an affront although he may lose by it, and be hissed at for a fool rather than engage in a sinful quarrel.

5. *It produces conformity to the best patterns.* To be meek is to be like the greatest saints. It is to be like the greatest angels. It is to be like God Himself who is slow to anger and in whom there is no fury.

### B. The Pleasure of a Meek and Quiet Spirit.

1. *The meek and quiet Christian enjoys himself.* Calm are the thoughts, serene are the affections, rational are the

prospects, and even and composed are the resolves of a meek and quiet soul. They are free from the pains and tortures of an angry man.

2. *The meek and quiet Christian enjoys his friends.* Man was intended to be a social creature and a Christian much more so. But the angry man is unfit to be so; he takes fire at every provocation. Meekness is the bond of Christian communion.

3. *The meek and quiet Christian enjoys God.* This is the quintessence of all happiness and that without which all our other enjoyments are sapless and insipid. "The meek also shall increase their joy in the Lord" (Isaiah 29:19).

4. *The meek and quiet Christian's enemies cannot disturb these enjoyments.* His enjoyment is not only sweet, but safe and secure. As far as he acts under the law of meekness it is above the reach of the assaults of those who wish ill to it.

## C. The Profitableness of a Meek and Quiet Spirit.

1. *It is the condition of a promise.* The meek are blessed for they shall inherit the earth (Matthew 5:5). It is not always the largest proportion of this world's goods that falls to the meek man's share, but whether he has more or less, he has it by the best title and he knows how to make a right and good use of it.

2. *It has a direct tendency to present benefit and advantage.* (a) Meekness has a good influence upon our health. Inordinate passions injure the body. (b) It has a good influence upon the preservation and increase of wealth. (c) It has a good influence upon our safety.

## D. The Preparative Value of a Meek and Quiet Spirit.

1. *It prepares for any duty.* It puts and keeps the soul in a frame for all religious exercises. We are fishers of men, but we seldom fish in troubled waters. Prayer is another duty for which meekness prepares us, as well as for the proper observance of the Lord's day and the Lord's Supper.

2. *It prepares for any relation to which God may call us.* Relations are various — superiors, inferiors, equals; he that is of a meek and quiet spirit is cut out for any of them. There are various duties and graces to be exercised; but meekness is the golden thread that must run through all.

3. *It prepares for any condition.* Whether the outward condition be prosperous or adverse, whether the world smile or frown upon us, a meek and quiet spirit is neither lifted up with the one nor cast down with the other, but always in the same poise.

4. *It prepares for persecution.* If tribulation and affliction arise because of the Word the meek and quiet spirit is armed for it, so as to preserve its peace and purity, that we may neither torment ourselves with a base fear nor pollute ourselves with a base compliance.

## CONCLUSION

The ornament I have been recommending to you is confessedly excellent and lovely; will you put it on and wear it, that by this all men may know that you are Christ's disciples?